THE ULTIMATE GUIDE TO
REAL ESTATE

THE ULTIMATE GUIDE TO

REAL ESTATE

John McGrath

HarperCollins*Publishers*

All investments carry risks. The views in this book are of a general nature only and do not take account of individual circumstances. You should always seek professional advice from qualified advisers before borrowing money and investing in property.

HarperCollins*Publishers*

First published in 2005 by HarperCollins*Publishers* Pty Limited
ABN 36 009 913 517
A member of the HarperCollins*Publishers* (Australia) Pty Limited Group
www.harpercollins.com.au

HarperCollins*Publishers*
25 Ryde Road, Pymble, Sydney, NSW 2073, Australia
31 View Road, Glenfield, Auckland 10, New Zealand
77–85 Fulham Palace Road, London W6 8JB, United Kingdom
2 Bloor Street East, 20th Floor, Toronto M4W 1A8, Canada
10 East 53rd Street, New York, NY 10022, USA

National Library of Australia Cataloguing-in-Publication data:

McGrath, John, 1963–.
    The ultimate guide to real estate.
    ISBN 0 7322 8086 9.
    1. Real property - Australia. 2. Vendors and purchasers -
    Australia. I. Title.
333.330994

Produced by Brewster Publishers Pty Ltd
Cover design by Ascender Design Practice, Sydney
Internal design by Brewster Publishers Pty Ltd
Typeset in 11.5/17pt AGaramond
Printed and bound in Australia by Griffin Press on 79gsm Bulky Paperback White

6 5 4 3 2 1   05 06 07 08

CONTENTS

INTRODUCTION

I'll never forget the day I took possession of my first property. It absolutely changed my life. After going through the process of borrowing the funds, finding a home to buy, negotiating the price and doing the legals, I was finally walking on my own floorboards. Knowing that I now had my own piece of real estate gave me a huge sense of fulfilment and happiness.

In my 22 years in the real estate industry, I've seen hundreds of people experience those same emotions when I've handed them the keys to their new home. I'm grateful to be able to share in their excitement and joy. I truly love my job. It feels fantastic to help a young couple into their first home, negotiate a deal for somebody's dream home or get a fantastic auction result for a vendor.

Wealth and lifestyle

A home is more than just the roof over our heads. It's the stage where our life's dramas are played out. It's where we raise our family, break bread with our friends and loved ones, and seek peace and solitude. We have some of the greatest moments of our lives within the four walls of our home.

For most Australians, their home is also their greatest source of wealth. So while having somewhere to live is the primary motivation of most people when buying a home, it's also important to understand the potential for wealth creation. As Henry Ford once said, 'One good real estate investment is worth a lifetime of toil'.

After I left school, when I was deciding on a career, I was reading the *Business Review Weekly* list of the richest Australians, looking for some inspiration. I noticed that about 75 per cent of them had built or consolidated their wealth by investing in property. So I understood from an early age that property is a fantastic foundation for wealth.

About this book

In this book I want to share my enthusiasm for property with you and give you some practical advice on buying, selling and investing in real estate. The book is divided into three sections: 'Buying', 'Selling' and 'Investing'.

In 'Buying' you'll learn how to research the market efficiently, find a home you love and buy it for the best price. I'll guide you towards the best home loan and share my negotiation tips and auction tactics.

The second section of the book is for people who are selling their homes. I explain the importance of choosing the right agent and how to maximise the sale price of your home.

In the final section I outline why I think property is one of the best investments for average Australians. I also share with you my simple strategy for building wealth with residential property.

Pleasure and profit

Owning property is a defining characteristic of our culture. Everyone wants to own their own little piece of Australia, and as a consequence we now have the highest rate of home ownership in the Western world. And while home buyers' tastes have broadened from a house on a quarter-acre block in the suburbs, the great Australian dream shows no sign of letting up.

In such a property-obsessed nation, most people have a reasonably high degree of knowledge around real estate already. But, by sharing the insights, tactics and strategies I've picked up over my time in the industry, I hope to give you an extra edge that will make your forays into property more pleasurable and profitable.

BUYING

LIFESTYLE

When you buy a home, you're buying much more than a patch of dirt and a roof over your head. What you're actually buying is a lifestyle. A home not only fulfils your material requirement for shelter, but it caters to your psychological, spiritual and lifestyle needs as well. The combination of the physical structure and its location create a lifestyle for you to enjoy. To put it another way, how you like to live should determine where you live.

For example, a brand new studio apartment in a chic development close to the CBD can give the owner an entrée into the inner-city café culture. It may appeal to young, fashion-conscious buyers who put a premium on their leisure time. With a busy working life and all the city's best boutiques, nightclubs, cinemas and bars at their doorstep, they may not have much time for home maintenance. The tiny kitchen isn't a drawback because there are a dozen restaurants and cafés within two blocks.

On the other hand, a home in the leafy suburbs promises a quiet and healthy environment for bringing up children. It would appeal to families who enjoy weekends relaxing by the pool or barbecues with friends. The suburb's not exactly hip, but the local butcher, baker and deli owner know you by name. The owners may consider a little maintenance here and there – a small price to pay for the beauty of the home's period features.

How do you want to live?

Before you decide what home to buy, give some thought to the lifestyle you prefer. Are you after a suburban family idyll? No-fuss, outdoorsy beach living? Inner-city excitement and convenience? Country-town simplicity and community? Or something else? What lifestyle suits your personal tastes and stage in life?

Broadly speaking, there are three elements that make up your 'property-lifestyle'.

Firstly there is the location of the property, which dictates the aspect and views the property enjoys, as well as the local amenities and the look and feel of the neighbourhood. Without a doubt, location is the home buyer's most important consideration, because you can always improve a home, but you can't improve a location. To a large extent, the location of the property also governs the capital growth of the property. Different suburbs and sectors of the property market appreciate at different rates and, by buying in an area primed for superior capital growth, you can build your personal wealth faster.

The second property-lifestyle element is the type of dwelling – freestanding house, terrace, townhouse, semi or apartment – which affects how you live in the space and the amount of upkeep required.

Finally, there are the financial and capital-growth aspects of the property, which have ramifications for your current and future prosperity.

Location, location ... and location

The time-honoured home buyer's adage is 'location, location, location'. But what actually makes a great location? A great location allows you to create the perfect lifestyle for you and your family. It's a combination of the physical location of the property, the character of the suburb and the proximity to desirable amenities.

Sometimes people get fixated on a particular street or a suburb, and this narrow focus means they can overlook some great opportunities. In the early stages of your home hunt, it's probably best to be a little bit curious about the many alternatives. After all, you can probably create your desired lifestyle in a number of locations.

When you're weighing up possible locations, there are a few issues to address. Are you near all the amenities you need, such as public transport, shops, schools, medical centres, and cafés and restaurants? Does the location have a pleasant streetscape and attractive housing stock? How long will it take to get to work? Is the suburb safe and quiet?

If you're considering buying in a suburb you're not familiar with, hang out there on weekends and at night-time. Have a meal in one of the popular restaurants, window-shop down the high street and have a stickybeak at the open-for-inspections. Could you feel at home here? Have coffee and get chatting to the locals. What do they like (and loathe) about the location?

When it comes down to choosing a particular property, you have to assess the aspect, the views and the outlook. You can always change the décor of a property, and you can often change the floor plan, extend or add another storey, but you can never change the location or the aspect. Home buyers will pay a premium for a northerly orientation of the main living, family and garden areas.

North-facing

You might be wondering why a northerly aspect is preferable. Well, in Australia the sun moves across the northern sky. So living areas, decks and balconies that face north or northeast receive plenty of natural light.

Lesson from *The Block*

I was fortunate to be selected as a judge on the first two series of Channel Nine's popular renovation-reality show *The Block*. My role was to go in every fortnight and judge which couple had added the most value to their apartment. The result in the second series illustrates the importance of a home's aspect.

Jamie and Andrew's winning apartment was on the bottom right of the four-unit building. It was on the northeastern corner and got plenty of sun. The runners-up, Jason and Kirsten, had the bottom-left apartment, which faced south. In my opinion, Jason and Kirsten had the best ideas and executed the best renovation. But they suffered from being south-facing, and I think that was the issue that beat them.

A HOME FOR EVERY LIFESTYLE

A house or a unit? For some buyers there's no decision to make. Many younger buyers have no time for mowing lawns or cleaning gutters – they want all their spare time for leisure activities. They're looking for a low-maintenance, security-focussed property with a cool, contemporary look in close proximity to cafés, nightclubs and restaurants. Clearly an apartment is going to fit the bill.

Other family-oriented buyers want green space for their children to roam around in. They want a home with character and features of yesteryear, and they're prepared to put a bit of effort into maintaining it. They have a good-sized budget and they're keeping an eye on future capital growth. For these people, a freestanding house is the best bet.

It's also a question of your personal taste. There are so many different styles of housing to choose from: Californian bungalows, Victorian terraces, Art Deco apartments, arts-and-crafts semis, P & O-style homes, fibro cottages and Queenslanders, just to name a few. What appeals to you?

For many buyers there's a bit of flexibility around what type of home they could live in. They're at least willing to consider the options. To help you get a feel for what's available, I've summarised the pros and cons of each of the various housing types.

Freestanding houses

If you own a freestanding house you really are master of your own domain. With no common walls, greater privacy and the least restrictions on renovating and extending, you have the most freedom to create your ideal habitat.

On a dollar-per-square-metre basis, freestanding houses are typically the most expensive type of dwelling. But the high entry price is offset by the superior capital growth houses have historically enjoyed.

Freestanding houses usually have more space than apartments and terraces, as well as gardens and outdoor living and entertaining areas. However, you bear the total burden for maintenance and upkeep, and council and water rates are typically higher.

Semi-detached houses

Semi-detached houses (or 'semis') have one wall shared with a neighbour and are usually found close to the inner city. The reason many people buy semi-detached houses comes back to price – they are a little more affordable than freestanding houses. But, because the house is attached on one side, you might want to choose your neighbours a bit more carefully.

Semis can be more difficult to extend because you've got your attached neighbours to negotiate with. They often have a lot of character and period architectural features, and there's usually a small garden out the back.

Townhouses and terraces

With a common wall on both sides, a townhouse or terrace is halfway between an apartment and a freestanding house. What you lose in privacy you make up for in extra space. They are usually bigger than units (although some terraces are tiny), and often have a garden or courtyard. Townhouses and terraces usually require less maintenance than a house and are often located close to the CBD.

I think terraces have terrific character, particularly Victorian-era stock, but because they're old, you need to be fairly careful when doing inspections. Rarely have I sold a terrace that hasn't had some degree of rising damp. It's not the end of the world, but you need to check it out and have a reasonable understanding of the cost of rectification.

Apartments and duplexes

When you buy an apartment, you are trading a portion of your privacy for reduced maintenance and the shared amenities – such as pools, tennis courts or security systems – that go along with apartment living. Apartments appeal to first home buyers because of their low entry price, and retirees because there's less maintenance required, with added security.

Apartments give you more 'bang for your buck' in that they are generally cheaper per square metre than houses. The body corporate is responsible for maintaining the building, so the financial burden of exterior maintenance is shared. Your options for renovating are often tightly controlled by the body corporate.

Because you have common walls and shared spaces, apartments have less privacy and more lifestyle restrictions than freestanding homes. However, apartment buildings sometimes have shared amenities such as pools and gyms, and often have increased security such as intercoms and security doors.

A duplex is a building divided into two apartments, usually one on top of the other, with separate entrances. If you buy the whole building, you have the advantage of home and income, or in-law, accommodation.

Going up

Apartment buildings just keep getting taller. The demand for inner-city living has encouraged developers to reach for the sky. As I write this, two 80-floor apartment buildings are under construction, one in Surfers Paradise and one in Melbourne. Sydney now has a 42-floor residential tower.

If you're considering high-rise living, there are a few factors you need to take into account. Generally speaking, you'll find developers add $10 000 to $20 000 per floor for an identical apartment as you go up

Houses vs apartments

Houses

Pros

- ✓ you're master of your own domain
- ✓ increased privacy
- ✓ no strata levies
- ✓ typically better capital growth
- ✓ few restrictions on renovations and extensions

Apartments

Pros

- ✓ body corporate takes care of exterior maintenance
- ✓ can have shared amenities e.g. pool or gym
- ✓ often better security

Houses

Cons

- ✗ more expensive per square metre
- ✗ you pay for all maintenance and must organise it yourself
- ✗ no strata levies

Apartments

Cons

- ✗ generally noisier
- ✗ generally smaller than houses
- ✗ restrictions on renovations
- ✗ little control over exterior of building

in the building. However, prestige developments may charge significantly more per floor – up to $100 000 extra per floor for otherwise identical apartments.

Given that the higher you go the more you pay, you must assess whether the extra height justifies the price. Does level 36 have a better view than level 28? I don't think that each floor necessarily has a better view than the one below. In fact, there comes a point where the view can deteriorate above a certain height.

If you go up really high, all you're going to see are clouds, sky and 'ants' scurrying around on the ground. That's fine, if that's what you like. But on the fourth floor you might get a view of a waterway, park or the cityscape.

Change your perspective

When you're assessing a property's views, sit down, because that's the position you'll actually be enjoying the view from most of the time. At inspections a lot of buyers will stand by windows ooh-ing and aah-ing over the view. But that's not where they're going to spend their time if they buy the home. So sit down in the dining and lounge areas and lie on the bed to get a realistic perspective of what you'll be looking at when you live there.

CAPITAL GROWTH AND FINANCIAL CONSIDERATIONS

The financial considerations of buying a home or investment property are perhaps the least obvious of the lifestyle elements of buying a property. But, since property makes up such a large proportion of our personal wealth, your purchase decision affects your future prosperity. The amount you spend, how much you borrow and the capital growth of your new property will all have a significant impact on your current and future lifestyle.

For example, would you prefer to forego some spending on clothes, a fancy car and eating out in the short term in order to acquire a bigger property or one in a more desirable location? Or would you prefer to maintain your easy-spending lifestyle and buy a more modest home, perhaps an apartment rather than a house, in a less salubrious area? Or perhaps you'd be better off continuing to rent and buying an investment property? There are usually some trade-offs to be made between your current spending and property ownership, especially when you're young.

Where does this property purchase fit into your life cycle? Perhaps you're keen to buy a starter home to get a foothold in the market. You may be willing to buy a run-down property and spend your weekends renovating to build your equity before trading up. Or, at the other end of the spectrum, perhaps you're downshifting into early retirement. In that case, you might be trading down from a family home to an apartment or semi, and using the surplus cash to fund your lifestyle.

First home buyers: short-term sacrifice, long-term gain

The first property I bought was a run-down inner-city terrace for $96 000. I cleaned it up bit and rented it out for $100 per week. Even though it wasn't a palace, it was a lot nicer than the $40-a-week studio apartment I was living in, which was a real dump. But I chose to stay there for another two years to maximise my cash flow so I could get a foothold in the market.

Looking back, I'm glad I made that sacrifice. A few years after I bought the terrace, I sold it for $260 000, and I thanked God I had been prepared to do it a bit tough for a couple of years. Because if I hadn't, I would have had to come up with a quarter of a million dollars to buy the same property.

Most markets are growing faster than you'll ever be able to save. So the question is not 'Should I get in?', but 'How can I get in?'. And if it's a bit tight at the moment, guess what? It's probably going to be tighter next year and the year after. So, work hard to find a solution today as to how you can get in the market. If you're living with your parents, maybe you can afford to buy a small investment property and continue to live at home for another couple of years while you build up some equity.

Where is your life going?

Before you buy a home, you need to look at how your lifestyle could change in the short term. Are you committed to the single life, or are you getting married and thinking about children? Is your family outgrowing your current digs, or will your children be fleeing the nest soon?

You need to think about your future needs, because buying the wrong home is a costly mistake to rectify. If you have to go through the process of selling one home and buying another, you'll pay around 10 per cent of the value of the home in exit and entry costs alone (such as stamp duty, agent's fees, marketing, removalists, etc).

If you are only planning to own the property for a short period, you must consider your exit strategy. Will the home be easy to sell when it's time to move on, or will it hang around the market like an albatross around your neck?

WEALTH AND PROSPERITY

The greatest source of wealth for most Australians is their home. Over the last decade private wealth in this country has more than doubled, largely driven by the booming property market. The average house price has more than doubled since 1996.

Since property makes up such a big part of our personal wealth, the astute buyer always keeps an eye out for potential capital growth. We all want to buy well and secure property that is primed to appreciate in value. However, not everybody is willing to spend the time researching the market to find the best buys.

Your property's capital growth not only boosts your personal wealth, it also creates a source of equity you can leverage to build your wealth even further. Unlocking the equity in your property by refinancing enables you to buy further capital-growth or income-producing investments. So the benefits of buying the right property are magnified as time goes on.

But sometimes there are trade-offs between potential financial performance and lifestyle considerations. You may be more than willing to pay over the odds for a property, or overcapitalise with renovations and extensions, to create a home that's tailored perfectly to your tastes, needs and lifestyle. After all, what is the value of the psychic income received from living in your dream home? It's hard to put a value on the pleasure of watching the sunset over the water from your balcony, or hearing your children's cheerful voices as they play in your beautiful garden.

Finance first

You've already got your finance pre-approved, right? Because I've seen

A prime location

What makes a great location depends on your lifestyle and needs. Consider the following factors:

✓ Is there a pleasant streetscape, view and aspect?

✓ Are there schools, shops, medical centres, cafés and restaurants nearby?

✓ What about beaches, parks and sporting facilities?

✓ How long does it take to get to work?

✓ What is the local community like?

✓ Is there car parking and public transport?

✓ Is there noise or pollution from traffic, aircraft or industry?

✓ Do you feel safe there after dark?

✓ Are you close to family and friends?

✓ Is there potential for better-than-average capital growth?

buyers find their perfect property early in their search, only to have it slip through their fingers because it's taken them a week to get their finance approved. A good property can be snapped up and off the market in a week. The average number of days on market in our company is around 30 – but that's the average. Many properties are sold within the first three or four days.

That's why it's so important to be on top of your game at all times. Nothing is more heartbreaking than missing out on your dream home because you're not fully prepared. To help you avoid disappointment, in the next chapter I explain how to get your home loan pre-approved .

GETTING YOUR FINANCE SORTED

The deregulation of the home-loan market in the early 1990s was one of the best things to ever happen to the property market in Australia. It led to a proliferation of mortgage providers that undercut the banks. The increased competition led to lower interest rates all round and more user-friendly home loans.

In the long run you will probably end up paying a lot less for your home by choosing the right home loan than by haggling the vendor down to the last $1000. That's because choosing the best mortgage could save you tens of thousands of dollars in unnecessary interest payments over the course of the loan.

RISKY BUSINESS

Whenever someone lends money, there's always a risk something could wrong and they won't get repaid. You would be cautious lending money to a complete stranger, and so are the mortgage providers. It's their business to reduce the risk of borrowers defaulting on their loans. So when you apply for a home loan, the lender's main concern is whether you're likely to repay it in full.

The key things they look for are the security of the loan, which comes down to the quality of the property you're buying, and your ability to repay the loan, which they judge by your track record for repaying previous loans and your employment record. If you've had four jobs in the last four years there'll be some concern about your employment stability and therefore your ability to maintain your loan repayments.

Not all security is equal

If worst comes to the worst and you can't repay your loan, your lender needs to be confident they can recover their money by selling the property you've provided as security for the loan.

The loan to value ratio (LVR) is the ratio of money borrowed to the amount of security given (i.e. the value of the home) expressed as a percentage. For example, if you borrow $250 000 and your home is worth $500 000, then your LVR is:

$$\frac{250\,000}{500\,000} \times 100 = 50\%$$

Most lenders are comfortable with an 80 per cent LVR. That means that you'll have to put up a 20 per cent deposit. If you want to borrow more than 80 per cent your lender usually requires you to have lender's mortgage insurance (LMI).

LMI makes up your lender if you can't pay back your home loan. If you default on the loan, it covers the shortfall between the proceeds from the sale of the property and the amount outstanding on your loan. The insurer will then try to reclaim this money from you.

If your lender thinks the home you want to buy is particularly risky, in a property downturn they may demand a higher LVR. Lenders prefer low-rise property in urban areas. For a lot of inner-city high-rise apartments or property in regional areas, many lenders require an LVR of 65 to 70 per cent.

Deposit

The first step in buying a home is saving a deposit. These days it's possible to borrow 100 per cent or more of the value of a property. But it's much easier to borrow money if you've got a deposit, and the bigger, the better. A 20 per cent deposit will be looked on favourably by your lender.

FINANCE BASICS

Before you choose a home loan, it's important to understand a few fundamental principles of finance and wealth building. First up, a couple of basic terms: the 'principal' is the amount you borrow; 'interest' is the lender's reward for lending you the money and is calculated as a percentage of the principal. The rate of interest your lender charges fluctuates over time, usually in line with official Reserve Bank of Australia interest rates.

Interest on your home loan is dead money. It's not tax-deductible and you have to pay it in after-tax dollars. So there's no reason to pay more than you absolutely have to – that will only delay your wealth-creation plans.

The amount of principal you must repay is set by your loan agreement. If you borrow $500 000 then you must repay $500 000. However, the amount of interest you pay back is totally up to you. If you want to minimise your interest you can, but if you choose to pay more, your lender will gladly accept it.

Home loan = saving discipline

Unless we're extremely disciplined, it's very easy to spend all the money we earn. So one of the beauties of buying property is that you have to pay the mortgage each month. I think it's a really terrific saving discipline.

Time is money

They say 'time is money', and that's especially true when it comes to paying off your home loan. There are many ways you can save money on your home loan, but they all boil down to one simple rule: the quicker you pay back the principal, the less money you pay overall.

Interest is levied on the principal outstanding. So by reducing the principal, you're paying interest on a smaller amount. Any payments made over and above the minimum repayment reduce the principal.

Time + interest
See how increasing the monthly repayment reduces the total amount of interest paid:

Monthly repayment	$2217	$2781
Time to pay off loan	25 years	15 years
Total interest paid	$365 092	$200 587
Interest saved	-	**$164 505**

Figures based on a $300 000 principal and interest loan at 7.5% interest over 25 years

By paying an extra $564 a month (or $130 a week), the loan in the example above can be paid off 10 years earlier, saving a whopping $164 505 in interest in the process. Another way to reduce the principal quickly is to make lump-sum payments whenever you can.

Principal and interest loans

There are several different kinds of home loans available, with various methods of repayment and combinations of features. Principal and interest (P & I) loans are most popular with home buyers.

The repayments are divided into a portion of interest and a portion to repay the principal. At the end of the loan, all the principal is repaid and you owe nothing. P & I loans are excellent for owner-occupiers because your equity increases as you pay off your principal.

In the early days of the loan, you pay very little off the principal – most of your repayments go to paying interest. The principal portion of your repayments slowly grows over the life of the loan. You pay off the bulk of the principal in the final years of the loan.

Principal + interest
Using the same figures as before, see how the principal portion of the loan repayments increases over time:

	End of year 1	End of year 10	End of year 25
Interest	$1851	$1499	$14
Principal	$366	$718	$2203
Total monthly repayment	$2217	$2217	$2217

Figures based on a $300 000 P & I loan at 7.5% interest over 25 years

---

Variable interest loans

There are three types of P & I loans, with the variable interest loan being the most popular. Your lender can increase or decrease the interest rate at their discretion. The interest rate is usually pegged to the official interest rates set by the Reserve Bank of Australia. These days, the home-loan market is very competitive and lenders usually only add a margin of between 1 and 2 per cent to the official rate.

You can choose the duration of the loan, up to 25 or 30 years, to suit your needs. A longer term will give you lower regular repayments, but you'll end up paying more in interest over the life of the loan.

The advantages of a variable home loan are that if the interest rate falls, so do your repayments. You can also make additional payments whenever you wish, so you can pay off the loan as quickly as you like without penalty, saving yourself a small fortune in interest.

There are two types of variable loans, with different interest rates and features. Standard variable loans are the most popular type of home loan in Australia. They are a flexible loan with useful features such as redraw facilities and offset accounts. Basic variable home loans are 'no-frills' loans. Their lack of features is compensated for by a lower interest rate.

Introductory rate loans

Some variable loans have what's called an introductory or honeymoon interest rate, which is lower than the normal variable rate and lasts for a short period – usually six months to two years. The introductory rate can be fixed, variable or capped. At the end of the introductory period, the rate reverts to a higher variable rate.

Introductory rates are usually the lowest on the market. The initial discount rate can give your wallet a bit of a break after having paid all the costs of buying your home. The catch is that, once the introductory rate is over, the variable rate is usually higher than the rate on standard variable loans, and you end up paying more in the long run.

Many people argue that introductory rates are nothing more than a marketing tool lenders use to get your attention. Ads with low rates in large type do tend to catch home buyers' eyes. But since legislation now requires lenders to advertise a comparison rate that reveals the true cost of the home loan, introductory rates have gone out of fashion.

Each-way bet

With a split (or combination) home loan you fix the interest of a portion of the loan and the balance is on the variable interest rate. These loans give you some security against rising interest rates while maintaining flexibility in relation to repayments. But they may have higher fees than a standard variable loan.

Fixed interest loans

With a fixed interest loan, the interest rate is set for the period of the loan. The amount of your repayments and the term of the loan are also fixed. The duration of the loan is usually between one and ten years, and at the end of that time you can repay the principal, roll over into another fixed term, or convert to the current variable interest rate.

If you want peace of mind, a fixed interest loan is the best way to go. You have the comfort of knowing exactly how much your repayments will be for the next few years. The drawback of fixed loans is that you usually can't make additional repayments to shorten the duration of the loan. If you want to pay off the loan early, you usually have to pay a substantial penalty. However, some fixed interest home loans now allow you to make extra repayments within certain limits.

Interest-rate insurance policy

When I've borrowed money to buy property I've consistently used variable interest rate finance. Most of the time the variable rate has been below the fixed rate, so I've been comfortable with that. But if I did sense that an upswing in interest rates was likely, or that I may have some issues with my cash flow in the medium term, I'd be locking in a fixed rate straightaway.

Looking back, fixed rates have been higher than variable rates over 80 per cent of the time. So if you're on fixed rates, you'll be paying a bit more in interest most of the time. However it's a small insurance premium that you can pay if you wish to plan your financial future. On fixed rates you have peace of mind, knowing that if you pick up the newspaper tomorrow and it says 'Interest rates up 1 per cent' that's not going to concern you too much.

Interest-only loans

As the name suggests, you only pay interest on an interest-only home loan. You don't make any contributions to paying off the principal during the course of the loan; you repay the principal in full at the end of the loan. The typical term is from one to ten years. When the loan expires, borrowers usually sign up for another fixed loan at the going interest rate.

Interest-only home loans are best suited to investors. Because you don't pay off any of the principal during the course of your loan, the regular repayments are less than a principal and interest loan. Thus you have more cash in your pocket, which allows you to borrow more and buy more property. Because the repayments are entirely interest, they are totally tax-deductible.

Line of credit

A line of credit is a bit like a big credit card secured by a mortgage on your property. As with a credit card, you have a pre-set limit and you can draw out funds whenever you like and for whatever you like. The big difference is that you pay interest at the lowest of all possible rates – the home-loan rate.

These loans have a lot of flexibility. You're only required to pay interest on the amount outstanding, although you can pay more to reduce the balance owing. Because the interest rates and fees are usually slightly higher than for regular principal and interest loans, though, they're not really suited to home buyers.

A line of credit is handy for investors because they can use it to put down deposits on new properties, pay for renovations or repairs, and cover short-term cash shortages. They can even buy a new property with the line of credit and find cheaper finance at their leisure.

CHOOSING A LOAN

When it comes to financing a property, a buyer's number one concern should be to get the cheapest loan possible. But with more than 150 lending institutions in Australia offering more than 3000 different home loans, each with a unique combination of interest rate, fees and features, finding the right mortgage to suit your budget, lifestyle and future plans can be a daunting task.

Paying the least amount of money over the course of your home loan comes down to two variables: the 'cost' of the loan (i.e. the interest rate and fees) and how quickly you can pay it back. While it's important to secure a low interest rate loan, you must ensure that your loan has the flexibility to allow you to pay it off sooner rather than later.

Lenders have come up with a range of ingenious features to help you pay back your loan as quickly as possible, saving you thousands in interest. The trick to choosing the right loan is to decide which features you must have and identify which loans offer these. Once you have a short list you can compare fees and interest rates and choose the cheapest loan.

Fee feast

The fees your lender charges are very important in determining the overall cost of the loan. Typical fees include:

Establishment fees (sometimes called application fees) – covers the administrative costs of setting up the loan.

Valuation fees – your lender will require a valuation of the property, usually at your expense.

Lender's solicitor's fees – covers the lender's solicitor's time spent preparing the mortgage documentation and often includes costs for searches to ensure the property is free of liabilities and not earmarked for reclamation by the government.

Periodic administration charges – these can amount to $20 a month or more.

Money-saving features

To help you be mortgage-free in the quickest possible time, your loan must allow you to make repayments at any time without penalty. To speed along the road to wealth, you'll want to pay as much spare cash as you can into your loan. You can make extra repayments, lump-sum payments and pay more than the minimum periodic repayments. You should not be penalised for doing so.

If you decide on a fixed interest rate loan, check that you can still make principal-reducing repayments during the fixed term. This is often possible, but your lender may apply limits to how much extra you can repay in a given period.

To streamline your financial management, your loan should also offer multiple methods of repayment to suit your lifestyle. Options include direct debit, salary credit, Internet banking and over-the-counter payments. You should also have the flexibility to make your repayments weekly, fortnightly or monthly.

Redraw facility

The best way to pay off your home loan as quickly as possible is to pay as much spare cash into it as you can. But what happens if you suddenly need that money for an emergency, such as unforeseen home repairs or a medical crisis? That's where a redraw facility comes in.

It allows you to redraw the extra funds you have paid into your loan above the minimum requirements. Many variable rate loans have a redraw facility and it's probably the most useful feature in a home loan. Your cash is available if you need it, but otherwise it's working to save you money on your loan.

Home loan interest is usually calculated daily and charged monthly. Every extra dollar you pay into your loan account reduces the amount of interest charged, even if it's in there for less than a month. So you want to keep the balance on your home loan as low as possible for as long as possible.

You can use a redraw facility like a savings account. Instead of being paid a low rate of interest in a bank account, you'll be saving a higher rate of interest by reducing your home loan principal. By storing any surplus funds in your home loan rather than your bank account, you end up paying less interest and you'll pay off your loan faster.

Comparison rates

Now you have a short list of loans which have all the money-saving features you want. They will probably have a range of interest rates and various fees you must pay. So how do you know which one is the cheapest?

The total cost of a loan is a combination of the fees and the interest rate. The benefits of a low interest rate can be easily wiped out by high ongoing fees. It might actually be cheaper to get a loan with a slightly higher interest rate and low or no fees than one with a lower interest rate and high establishment and ongoing fees.

The easiest way to compare one loan with another is to look at the Annualised Average Percentage Rate (AAPR), commonly known as the comparison rate. It is calculated to indicate the 'true' cost of the loan by combining the interest rate with the fees and charges and averaging them out over the course of the loan.

Under the Uniform Consumer Credit Code, any advertisement for a loan which contains an annual interest rate must also contain a comparison rate. When you're doing your home loan research, you can ask lenders for their comparison rate schedule. *Your Mortgage* magazine is also a great source of information on home-loan comparison rates and is available in most newsagents.

Compare apples with apples

Comparison rates indicate the cost of the loan, not its benefits. So when using comparison rates, it's important to only compare loans with similar features. Loans with interest-saving features such as redraw facilities or offset accounts usually have higher comparison rates than basic loans. But their greater flexibility will allow you to pay the loan off faster and save more money in the long term.

I NEED HELP!

With so many different loans available, each with a different interest rate and combination of fees and features, choosing the best loan can be a daunting task – especially for first-time borrowers. If you're feeling overwhelmed, don't worry – a mortgage broker can guide you through the mortgage maze.

Mortgage brokers help you choose an appropriate loan from their panel of lenders and assist with the application process. They are paid a commission by the lender, which varies from lender to lender. Their services are usually free to borrowers, and they can be a real time saver.

The broker collects all your relevant information at an interview, which can often be conducted at your home. Once they know your financial situation and risk and lifestyle preferences, they can find a loan to fit your needs using their product knowledge and dedicated software.

Using the software, the broker can show you comparisons of the features, fees, repayment schedules and interest rates of suitable loans, so you can make an informed choice. Brokers are familiar with lenders' approval criteria, so they can steer you towards a loan that you are more likely to get approved.

The bad old days

It's the best time ever in the history of Australia to be shopping around for finance. I remember when I went to my bank manager to get my first mortgage. I was petrified. In those days the culture was very conservative, the power was in the hands of the lenders, and my bank manager was an intimidating figure with a three-piece suit and long sideburns. Young people weren't considered particularly good prospects for home loans.

Up until about ten years ago, borrowers were generally treated poorly and you were made to feel lucky even to get an appointment with your bank manager. With the deregulation of the finance sector and the rise of the mortgage-broking industry, all that has changed. The competitiveness for new loans is the highest it's ever been, and there are lenders out there fighting to get your business. Assuming you're not a high-risk borrower, you're probably going to have any number of lenders wanting to put your loan on their books.

The great thing about mortgage brokerage firms is that they're like travel agents. Their fees are in-built into every loan that's on the market, so it doesn't cost you a cent to tap into an expert's opinion to assess the overall market. I think you'd be crazy to sign up for a mortgage without talking to a broker first. Because it's not going to cost you anything, there's no obligation, and they'll find the cheapest loan for your situation.

I recently suggested a friend of mine talk to a broker from our in-house mortgage brokerage, Oxygen Home Loans, because she wanted to finance a new investment property. The broker took a look at the current finance on her property portfolio and refinanced those loans, which saved her $10 000 a year, as well as getting her a great deal on a loan for her new property.

Take precautions

The mortgage broking industry has boomed in the past few years. But it's largely unregulated, and after several reports of unconscionable conduct there's now pressure from ASIC (Australian Securities and Investment Commission) for greater regulation. You need to take precautions to ensure you're dealing with a reputable broker.

I would recommend choosing a broker who is a member of the Mortgage Industry Association of Australia. You can find a list of members at www.miaa.com.au. Ask how big the broker's panel of lenders is. The bigger the panel, the better your chances of securing a good deal. The panel should have 20+ lenders.

To avoid bias, you need to ask about commissions the brokers receives from different lenders. Be careful your broker isn't steering you towards a loan for which they will receive a bigger commission, rather than one that will best suit your needs. Avoid brokers who want to charge you a fee for their services.

Caveat emptor

A mortgage broker can save you a lot of time and hassle, but you need to reassure yourself that you're happy with the deal. Some of the best and cheapest home loans are sold by lenders direct to the public, but you'll have to do the legwork to find them.

APPLYING FOR A LOAN

When you apply for a loan, the lender wants to get an overall picture of your financial position to see if you're a good bet for repaying their loan. Their main concern is your ability to make the regular repayments. It's not a question of how many assets you own, but how much you can afford to pay each month.

You'll need to provide the lender with evidence of all your income, assets, debts and current expenditure. Here's a check list of what you'll need:

Income

* evidence of your salary – usually two recent pay slips and the last two years' group certificates

* if you're self-employed, you'll need to show your last two tax returns

* details of any investment income from shares or property.

Assets

Details of the assets you own including:

* investments

* bank accounts

* life insurance and superannuation policies

* other assets such as cars and jewellery.

Expenditure

Details of your monthly expenses:

* living expenses – food, utilities, petrol, clothing, etc.

* child-support payments.

Liabilities

Details of any debts you have, such as:

* car loans

* personal loans

* credit and charge card limits

* other home loans.

Home loan hurdles

The major lending criteria for a home loan are as follows:

* stable income and good employment history, or continuous income if you're self-employed

* a good deposit – 20 per cent or more is preferable

* quality property to put a mortgage on – lenders like low-rise homes in major urban centres

* a good credit history

* guarantors – if you have problems with any of the above.

LET'S GO SHOPPING!

If your loan application is successful, your lender will give you a home-loan guarantee certificate or a pre-approval certificate. This means your home loan will be approved when you find a home you want to buy, provided you meet a few conditions. You can start home hunting with confidence, knowing exactly how much you've got to spend.

The most important condition of final approval is that the loan amount is based on the bank's valuation of the property, not on the purchase price. This is a crucial point that's sometimes overlooked by buyers. If you pay more than the bank thinks the home is worth, you'll have to make up the shortfall between the selling price and the bank's valuation.

Home loan pre-approvals don't last forever either. They are typically valid from three to six months. If yours is about to run out and you still haven't found your dream home, call the lender and ask if you can have it extended, or whether you need to reapply for the loan.

Strictly business

If you get knocked back for a loan, try not to take it personally. It just means you don't fit the lender's criteria – it's not a slur on your character. Consult a couple of mortgage brokers about your prospects with other lenders. It's also a good idea to check your credit rating just in case there's a problem you're not aware of.

BUT WAIT ... THERE'S MORE

Aside from your home loan and deposit, there are a few other significant costs of buying a home that you'll need to factor into your budget. It costs around 5 per cent of the purchase price to cover all the extras such as stamp duty, removalists and reports.

✳ Stamp duty

You have to pay stamp duty on the purchase price of the home. This is the biggest add-on expense for home buyers. You also have to pay stamp duty on your mortgage.

✳ Pre-purchase inspections

You need building and pest reports before you sign on the dotted line. If you're buying an apartment, you should also get a strata report.

✳ Conveyancing fees

You need to pay a solicitor or conveyancer to arrange the legal transfer of title. You also have to pay to have the transfer of title registered with the state land titles office.

✳ Removalists

You can pay anything from $200 to $20 000, depending on how much furniture and chattels you own.

TAKING IT TO THE STREET

Now that your finances are in order, you can start home hunting in earnest. While on one level you're looking for the perfect home, what you're really doing is simply gathering information. At first you're just getting a feel for the market – what's available, what you like and dislike, what different locations have to offer, and what you can get for your money.

You're learning about what suburbs and what streets you can afford, what different neighbourhoods look like, what the traffic and public transport situation is, and the quality of the shops and cafés. You're discovering what style of home you'd like to live in, and you're finding out exactly where you'd like to live and how much it will cost to buy a home there.

As you start attending open-home inspections, you'll also be able to take the temperature of the market in terms of how much stock is listed for sale, how many buyers are vying for properties, how long homes are taking to sell and what the level of demand is.

Once you get a bit clearer on what's available and what you'd like to buy, you start to narrow your search down to particular types of houses in particular suburbs (or even particular streets in particular suburbs). As you gather more information, your knowledge of these 'micro markets' becomes very precise and you'll develop excellent instincts for how much properties will sell for.

Five steps to finding your new home

The challenge of finding a new home is to create a plan to bridge the gap between where you're living now and the new home you'd like to own. If you follow my five-step plan, you can find a home you love at the right price:

1. Have a positive attitude – house hunting can be fun and exciting if you maintain a positive attitude.

2. Write a wish list – if you don't know what you're looking for, how will you know when you've found it?

3. Choose your preferred suburbs – start wide, then narrow down your search to a few suitable neighbourhoods.

4. Work out what you can afford – make sure you can afford a home that meets your wish list in your top suburbs.

5. Attend open inspections – you can test the temperature of the market as you view suitable homes.

LET'S GET EXCITED

Some people find looking for a property to buy a stressful experience. It's a very expensive purchase, and there's always the worry that you might not find anything you like in your price range. Plus there's a competitive aspect to it. There are usually a few other buyers you'll need to beat to the jump to secure a good property. And if it's an auction, you must brave the intensity of competitive bidding.

But rather than getting stressed out, I advise you to get excited about the prospect of owning your new home. Focus on all the benefits and enjoyment you'll get once you've moved in, because I find the people who do best at home hunting are the ones who get really excited about the process. They're enthusiastic about finding the right home and they relish the thrill of the chase.

Positive attitude

If you're optimistic that you'll find a property that meets all your requirements at a price you can afford, you're very likely to find it. However, if you're convinced that property is overpriced, all vendors are greedy and all real estate agents are sharks, it will be hard to maintain the motivation required for a successful home hunt.

Beware the media's often exaggerated boom-or-gloom stories about the property market. If you believe everything that's written, you'll convince yourself it's never the right time to buy. It's natural to be cautious when you're spending such a large amount of money, but researching current market values will go a long way to ensuring you buy at the right price.

You don't need any specialist skills or above-average intelligence to buy a good property. If you follow the advice I have given you in this book, research the market thoroughly and make sure you do your due diligence, you should be able to buy the right property at the right price.

HOME WISH LIST

There's an old saying: 'If you don't know where you're going, any road will take you there'. What this means in terms of your home hunt is that, if you don't set some parameters on what you're looking for, you'll waste a lot of time inspecting properties that aren't suitable for your needs or budget.

To make your home hunt efficient, you need to limit your search to suburbs and homes that are likely to provide the lifestyle you're seeking. As you go through the process of buying a home, you'll need to make a series of interrelated decisions based on your budget and lifestyle priorities. For example, if you want to live within walking distance of your CBD office, chances are you'll be buying an apartment or perhaps a terrace on the city fringe.

Or, if you need a five-bedroom, three-bathroom home for your growing family, and you'd like a pool and maybe a tennis court, you'll probably be looking at more affluent suburban locations. If your budget is limited, you may have to be more flexible about location and housing style, and might consider a run-down property than needs some TLC.

Compromises may have to be made. If you want to live in a highly sought-after location, you may have to settle for a smaller house or an apartment. If you want a large home on a large block, you might have to move a little further from the inner city than you'd like. You might settle for a smaller home to be closer to work or to your friends and family.

Remember, you're buying a lifestyle. You should spend some time considering how you'd like to live your life and then set about finding a property where you can create that lifestyle within the budget you have to spend.

We'll start to define the parameters of your home hunt by drawing up a wish list of the features of your ideal home.

Which home?

Choosing the desired features of your new home comes down to working out what your needs and long-term goals are. Here's a list of things to consider:

Feature	Considerations
Dwelling type	Are you flexible about the type of home you can live in or do you have your heart set on a house or an apartment?
Style	Would you prefer a contemporary or period home?
Aspect	North-facing is preferable, but can you live without it?
Bedrooms	How many bedrooms do you need?
Size	What size home do you need to accommodate all your possessions?
Bathrooms	One bathroom or two? Do you need a bath? Would you like a guest bathroom and/or en suites?
Car parking	Do you require a garage or off-street parking? For how many cars?
Kitchen	Separate or eat-in? Do you require a dishwasher?
Dining room	Do you want a separate dining room or will an eat-in kitchen do?
Entertaining areas	Do you prefer separate formal entertaining areas or more contemporary open-plan entertaining areas? How big?
Study/home office	Will you be working from home?

Interior features	Would you like carpets, polished floorboards, a fireplace, ornate plaster ceilings, air conditioning?
Leisure facilities	Do you want a pool, tennis court or billiards room?
Outdoor areas	Would you like a garden or outdoor entertaining area?
Storage	Do you need room to store your lifestyle or hobby equipment?
Renovations/extensions	Do you want to just move in or are you prepared to renovate or make additions to create your dream home?

As you think about your ideal home, it's a good idea to sort out your needs from your wants. Your needs are the 'must-have' features, while your wants are a bonus or a 'wouldn't it be nice if …'. Unless you have an unlimited budget, you can't always afford everything you want. But you can most likely afford a home that meets all your needs.

Write up your home wish list in point form. Run it by all the members of your household to make sure you agree on the basic requirements. Having a written list gives you a benchmark to evaluate potential homes against, and helps you focus your energy on finding the right home.

While it's great to be clear about what sort of home you're looking for, don't be too inflexible about your list of must-have features. Try to keep an open mind to different possibilities. I've seen buyers reject a home because it didn't have every single item on their wish list, only to end up regretting it six months later because they hadn't seen anything better.

WHICH SUBURB?

Most buyers already have a short list of locations they'd prefer to live in. These are often those familiar suburbs where you've spent time with friends and family. It's not too hard to imagine yourself living there.

But, having given some thought to the lifestyle you'd like your home to provide, I would advise you to begin your home hunt by considering a fairly wide range of suburbs. I always say to buyers, 'Keep a fairly open view as to where you're going to buy'.

Often buyers get stuck on one particular suburb and won't look anywhere else. For example, a young couple looking for their first home fall in love with the bohemian café culture and cute terraces and semis of one particular inner-city suburb. So they don't look anywhere else. But in reality there are probably several other locations in the city that have the same mix of housing stock and lifestyle. There could be a property two suburbs away from where they're looking that's perfect for them and a great buy, but they miss out because their search is too narrow.

The hallmarks of a good neighbourhood are:

* good schools

* low crime rate

* well-maintained homes

* a balance of housing styles

* desirable local amenities – parks, beaches, wide streets, shops and eateries, attractive streetscape, sporting and entertainment facilities

* a settled community – no big developments on the drawing board (unless they're good!).

In the early stages of your home hunt it's best to keep an open mind about where you might live, and investigate all the alternative locations where you can create your desired lifestyle. When you're auditioning new suburbs, walk around to get a feel for area. Have a coffee in the local café and chat to locals about what's good and bad in the area.

WHAT CAN YOU AFFORD?

Now that you've got your home wish list and investigated a few suitable suburbs, it's time for a reality check. What can you actually afford to buy?

Your lender will tell you how much they're willing to lend you. But they can't tell you how much money you will be comfortable paying off the loan each month. Have a look at your budget and see what repayments you can realistically afford. Are you willing to rein in your lifestyle spending in order to own a new home?

And don't forget to take into account the buying costs (such as mortgage application fees, stamp duty, removalists, etc.) plus any repairs or renovations required to make the place habitable. You'll also need to budget for all the ongoing costs of owning your new home, such as council and water rates, insurance, maintenance and upkeep, and body corporate fees.

Once you've calculated the realistic amount you have to spend, you can use one of the real-estate Web portals (such as realestate.com.au or domain.com.au) to see what you'll get for your money. Go to the search section and enter your preferred suburbs and budget. You can then view a range of homes for sale in your preferred location and price range. If you like what you see, great. If not, you may have to look for alternative locations.

Future needs

Make sure you take into account your future needs. Is this a starter home that you'll sell in the short term? If so, you should work out your exit strategy and choose a home that's going to be easy to sell. You might also be willing to settle for a less than perfect home or a fixer-upper that you can add value to by renovating.

Will you be getting married or starting a family soon? If so, you'll probably need a bigger home with a garden. Do you have the skills, finance and patience to renovate or extend a home? Given your long working hours, are you really going to have dinner parties in a separate dining room, or is that just wishful thinking?

HOME HUNTING WEAPONS

H ome hunting is not a spectator sport. If you're committed to finding a great home at the right price, you have to get off the couch and into the marketplace. You have to go to open-home inspections, get to know a few agents, walk the neighbourhood and take notes in your inspection notebook. You have to attend auctions, record sales data, read the papers and keep your finger on the pulse of the market.

In this chapter, I have outlined some of the best tips and techniques that I've seen buyers use to find a home they love, sooner rather than later, and for the right price. From my experience, the people who find and buy the best properties in the shortest time frame are the ones who really immerse themselves in the search. They make it their part-time job until they've exchanged contracts on their dream home. Buyers who dabble a bit here and there often end up struggling to find what they're looking for. It's hard to get a feel for the market from the sidelines because it can change quite rapidly.

LET YOUR MOUSE DO THE WALKING

With advances in Internet technology, home hunters today have more information about the property market than ever before. Real estate websites offer unparalleled access to listings of homes for sale and historical sales data, as well as powerful search tools that enable buyers to sift through the entire market.

You can search through a large part of the market without even leaving your home. Images, floor plans and even virtual tours are all available online. You can usually contact the agent via e-mail to get further information. It's never been easier or more convenient to find a home to buy.

Many real estate websites have e-mail property alerts. You register your details and nominate your preferred property style, suburbs and price range, and you'll be notified every time a home meeting your criteria is listed for sale. Around 20 per cent of people who buy through our company are introduced to the property via an e-mail alert. They registered their buying criteria on our website, and we kept sending them property alerts until they found the right one.

Some agents' sites will even update you every week on what properties they've sold and how much they went for. Using the Web is definitely the most convenient and efficient way to keep up to date on the market.

OTHER SOURCES OF LISTINGS

The other sources of for-sale listings are the metropolitan and local newspapers and real estate magazines. Obviously local papers and magazines have the advantage of pictures, so you can get a good idea of what the property looks like. But don't neglect the metropolitan papers' real estate sections, as there are usually a few gems lurking amongst the classifieds, especially at the budget end of the market.

As you're driving around doing your inspections, keep an eye out for fresh signboards. If the property makes a favourable first impression, take a note of the agent's details and follow it up. A drive-by inspection is an efficient way to rule out unsuitable properties. If the home doesn't feel right at first glance, you might want to give it a miss. But don't be too hasty, because a dilapidated-looking property might be a diamond in the rough.

One last way to find homes for sale is to actually knock on doors and ask owners if they are (or would) consider selling. It's not for everyone, and you can expect a lot of funny looks and rejections. But it's a good strategy if you have your heart set on a particular street or location.

Be prepared

Open-home inspections are a great way to research the property market. You can often see 10 or 15 properties in quick succession on a Saturday, to give you a first impression of what's available and what you can buy for your money. And hopefully you're having fun and gathering a few interior-decorating ideas along the way!

There are two pieces of equipment that are essential for all home hunters. The first is a map of your preferred suburbs. You can make one by photocopying pages from your street directory and sticky-taping them together. As you do your inspections, mark important information on the map, such as streets you like and don't like, and the locations of schools, shops, cafés and public transport.

If you speak to the agents and locals as you do your inspections, you can pick up loads of valuable information, such as which areas are more affordable and which are premium priced, and which areas are undesirable due to local climate and geographical conditions, pollution from transport and industry, high crime or bad-news neighbours.

Inspection notebook

The second thing you'll need is something to record all your notes and information in. Create an inspection notebook to record information about all the homes you inspect. You can use an A4 pad and a clipboard, a loose-leaf binder or a big scrapbook.

When you inspect a property, write down its address, the agent's contact number and any information you think will be useful. You can sketch the floor plan and make notes on what you like and don't like about the property, list possible repairs and renovations. File the brochure the agent gives you along with your notes.

Be sure to note the asking or expected auction price. Once the property is sold, you can follow up with the agent to see how much it went for. Alternatively, most weekend metropolitan newspapers and some real estate websites publish recent sales results.

A bit of forward planning will save you a lot of time and stress when you're home hunting. On Friday night you can start drawing up an open-homes timetable from promising listings you've found in the newspaper and on the Internet. Mark the locations of the properties you want to inspect on your map. If you get up early on Saturday morning, you can add the latest listings from the morning's paper. Once you've browsed the property classifieds and downed your morning coffee, it's time to hit the streets.

SHORT-LISTING HOMES

Once you've got a feel for what's on offer in the current market and you've settled on a few preferred suburbs, it's time to start short-listing homes to buy. As you get more into buying mode, you'll be inspecting homes more carefully, seeing how they compare to your wish list and keeping an eye out for any obvious defects or other issues that will influence your offers or decision to buy.

Initially you're just getting a feel for the property and seeing if you could feel at home there. At this stage you don't have to make a comprehensive assessment of the structural integrity or the quality of the electrical wiring and plumbing. There will be time for that later (and it's best left to the professionals anyway).

Your first query is whether this home will fit your lifestyle. Does it correspond to your wish list (with at worst a few compromises)? Do you have a good feeling about the home and can you easily imagine yourself living there?

Does the home have a flowing and workable layout? A good layout creates easy living, convenience and privacy. How are the living areas situated in relation to the bedrooms? And where are the bathrooms in relation to the bedrooms?

Is there enough room for your family and possessions? Is there enough storage space? Is there potential to extend or reconfigure the layout to meet your requirements? What is the condition of the interior? Are any renovations necessary? Pay careful attention to the kitchen and bathroom, as these are the most expensive rooms to upgrade.

Does the home admit enough natural light for your liking? Be aware that it's customary to turn all the lights on for inspections and to time the inspection when the home is most light-filled. Switch the lights off to get an accurate indication of the home's brightness. Natural light is a much bigger consideration in apartments and attached houses than in freestanding homes.

Check the aspect of the home. If you're not too *au fait* with the local geography, take a compass with you to check which direction the living areas face. Is the home close to the local amenities, but not too close to pubs, industry, noisy transport routes and busy roads?

The wow factor

Does the home have something special – a 'wow factor' that makes you want to own it from the moment you walk in the front door? A high level of intrinsic appeal is a bit of a double-edged sword. It probably means the home will be in demand, which means that it won't sell for a bargain. But it will be more likely to retain its value than run-of-the-mill properties.

Try to be discerning. Remember, the home has been styled to look its absolute best. Is the wow factor being created by the chic furnishings and fresh flowers? Will it look as good when all your furniture is in there? Try to make an objective assessment of all the home's pluses as well as its shortcomings.

Don't overdo it

Be wary of trying to looking at too many properties in one day. After a while, all the homes start to blend together and you won't be able to give your full attention to features that might make you fall in love with the home.

Inspection check list

As you do your inspections, it's important to take notes to help you assess and compare all the properties you've seen. Here's a check list to prompt you on all the vital facts and figures you should jot down:

* address of property

* asking price or agent's indication

* agent's phone number

* number of bedrooms

* number of bathrooms

* general condition of property

* aspect and natural light

* any noise or pollution issues

* any repairs and renovations needed

* what fittings are included

* proximity to amenities

* what I really like about this property

* what I don't like about this property.

If you're buying a fixer-upper, it's a good idea to note down the dimensions of the rooms. You'll then be able to estimate the amount of materials (floor coverings, paint, etc.) you need to buy and create an approximate budget of renovation costs.

If you have a digital camera, you can take photos of the property, especially of details and features you like. They will help you to review all the properties you've seen when the day is over.

What to ask the agent

Here are a few useful questions to ask the agent:

* How many contracts are out?

* Why is the owner selling?

* Have the owners bought elsewhere?

OBVIOUS DEFECTS

Before you exchange contracts, I strongly recommend you get a professional building and pest inspection done (I'll discuss that more in the next chapter on due diligence). You should always be on the lookout for any signs of obvious defects. If you identify any major problems, it may be best to give that property a miss. At the very least, you'll save yourself the cost of a building report and possibly avoid costly and time-consuming rectification work.

Defects

Things to look out for include the following:

* Check the power board in the electricity box. If it's relatively new (especially if it has a circuit breaker), that's good. If the board is in original condition, it could indicate that the home is due for rewiring.

* Sagging floors (check near fireplaces) or moving floorboards can indicate problems with the stumps or bearers.

* Are the walls flat, straight and free of cracks? If not, the foundations may be shifting.

* Dark stains around the skirting boards can indicate rising damp. That's not necessarily a deal breaker, but you need to get it checked out.

* Turn on a tap in the bathroom and check the water pressure (hot and cold). If it's weak, there may be problems with the plumbing.

* Is the roofline sagging? The trusses or the entire roof may need replacing.

* Stains on the ceiling or rafters indicate there's a leak in the roof.

* Is the underfloor area well ventilated and free of signs of termites?

* Are the foundations free of cracks? Cracked foundations can lead to uneven floors and cracks in walls.

* Is recent painting covering up any defects?

Don't be afraid to ask questions. The agent is there to help you. Simple questions can reveal issues that you hadn't thought of previously. Better to look stupid asking a question than be saddled with a home with a whole lot of problems. And always keep an ear out for what other buyers are saying about the property at the inspection. They may have seen something you've missed.

NEW KIDS ON THE BLOCK

I'm always surprised by how few buyers check out the neighbourhood they're about to move into. A lot of people buy a property after one or two inspections. They check out the home, ask how much it is, and maybe bring their partner for a look. Then all of a sudden they're in negotiation mode.

The agent and vendor have a vested interest in showing a property at the time of day that best shows the property off. That's only natural. However, from a buyer's point of view, you want to make sure that at other times it's an equally pleasant environment. So if the home is near a school, a retail strip or a sporting facility, you want to know if that will have any impact on the way you're going to live.

I think it's important to spend a little time getting to know the area. Walk around the location and sit outside in your car at different times of the day and days of the week – at night, in the morning, on weekends, during the week, peak hour, after school, when the local pub is closing, etc. How is the street parking situation? In the inner city, finding a park on the street is usually difficult. Will you and your visitors be able to park your cars?

It's also a good idea to find out who your neighbours are going to be, especially if you're buying an apartment. If you spend a little bit of time around the property, it will be easy to meet the locals. It's amazing what you can pick up on the grapevine. You might find out about local traffic conditions, problem neighbours, noise issues and proposed developments.

WORKING WITH AGENTS

Because agents are paid by the vendor, traditionally they have focussed more on servicing their clients rather than helping buyers find the right property. But times are changing. Good agents understand that they need to build relationships with buyers in order to bring the deal together. A sale doesn't happen until they've got a buyer and a seller.

Switched-on agents will have a buyer strategy as well as a seller strategy. If you're a motivated buyer with your finance approved, they will be happy to help you find a home. So an excellent way to turbo-charge your home hunt is to build relationships with a few agents and brief them on the type of property you'd like to buy.

Some real estate experts might question this approach. A lot of people will tell you that agents are not necessarily a buyer's friend, and you should be a bit cagey about what you tell them – especially how much money you're willing to spend. Given that the agent's job is to get the highest price for the property, it may not be a good idea to reveal your hand, they say.

Don't be naïve about it – at the end of the day you have to accept that the agent *does* work for the vendor, and their job is to negotiate the best price for them. But that doesn't mean they can't help you too.

The price is right?

You must realise that when it's negotiation time, the onus is definitely on you to satisfy yourself that the price is right. You can't just accept the fact that the agent tells you the price is right. You need to do your due diligence and make your own assessment of value.

If you strike up a relationship with the right agent, I think you can be pretty open with them. The challenge is that if you hold your cards too close to your chest, you run the risk of not finding out about some good property. For example, you might tell the agent, 'I have about $300 000 to spend', but you really have $375 000 and you don't want them to know your final limit.

The agent might have a property that's on their books at $400 000, but they know the owner will probably take an offer at your upper limit. It's in your interest to hear about that. So I think you're better off being open with the agent, but you must do your own checking before you sign any contracts.

More coverage

Working with a few agents gives you more coverage of the market. Each agent can usually access all of the listings for their office, so once you've briefed one agent on your requirements, they can introduce you to a range of properties handled by their colleagues. They can also tell you about property that's just been listed but hasn't been advertised yet. In most real estate companies, you'll find around 20 per cent of the property they have for sale is not marketed or advertised.

Choose the key agents in your area who have a good market share and with whom you feel you can build rapport. When you're doing your inspections, you'll quickly get a feel for who the proactive agents are.

If you develop a good a relationship with an agent, they should keep you up to date on new listings that you might be interested in. Realistically, though, the onus is probably on you to keep in regular contact with the agent. Agents do get very busy, and they're probably dealing with a large number of buyers. Your brief can sometimes slip off their radar. Unfortunately it happens.

Make a list of the phone numbers of the agents you deal with and give them a call every fortnight. Just touch base, remind them that you're still looking, and check if anything has come in that they might not have let you know about.

It's also helpful to update your agents if your brief changes. Perhaps you've been looking for a few months and realise you can't get a property you'd like for the amount of money you have to spend. So you've been to your lender and arranged to borrow another $50 000. Give the agents you're working with a call and let them know, because it will help them to find you the right home.

Market barometer

I advise home hunters to attend as many auctions as they can. Auctions are a fantastic barometer of what the market's doing. They're a very easy way to get an understanding of what property values are doing in real time. And also, when you finally attend an auction for a property you want to bid on, if you've already been to a few you'll be less nervous about bidding.

BECOME A SUBURB EXPERT

After a few weekends of inspections, your home hunt should be starting to get more precise. You begin focussing closely on your two or three preferred suburbs and the types of homes that fit your wish list and budget.

It makes sense to limit your search to a particular type of property in your preferred suburbs, because it's easier to keep abreast of values and what's available. At this stage of the game, you need to develop an extensive knowledge of recent sales and a keen sense of value. Because if you're not a suburb expert on property values, you could easily make an expensive mistake.

Start by getting a suburb report from Australian Property Monitors or Residex. These companies collate property sales data and compile it into reports for buyers. For less than $100, you can get price data on all properties sold in a suburb (or postcode) over the last twelve months. With your report in hand, you can drive or walk around your chosen suburbs and see what homes in your price range have sold recently.

Follow up on all the homes you have inspected and find out how much they sold for. You can call the agent, or most weekend metropolitan newspapers and some real estate websites publish recent sales results. Note down the prices in your inspection notebook.

After a few weeks of looking, you'll be able to make an informed assessment of what a property is worth. You'll know what features are fairly standard in the properties in your price range, and how much extras (such as a garage, extra bedroom or view) are likely to add to the price. You'll know how much demand there is and what the most recent prices are. In short, you'll know a good buy when you see it.

Detailed inspections

Once you've found a few properties you like, you can put them down on your short list for more detailed inspections before you start making offers. First up, you must confirm that the home has all your must-haves. Also, take your time in going over the property for signs of any structural problems.

Next, you have to see if there are any problems with the location that wouldn't be apparent during inspection times. There are a few issues that can have a big impact on your lifestyle and usually require additional research before you can make an informed decision.

The first is commuting time. If you have an aversion to peak-hour traffic, it's a good idea to drive the route to your work on a weekday morning to find out how long it takes. If you'll be using public transport, stop by the train station or bus stop and ask the commuters how long it actually takes to get to your destination. If the property you're looking at doesn't have any parking, drive by after work and see how hard it is to get a park on the street.

Noise can be a big issue, especially if there are eateries, pubs or nightclubs nearby. Take a walk around the neighbourhood and make a note of any late-night businesses and their closing times. If noise is a critical consideration for you, do another walk around late at night when patrons will be moving onto the street. You could also call the local police station and see if there are any noise problems with the street the home is located in.

The amount of natural light in a home has a profound effect on the atmosphere, which in turn affects the mood of the occupants. Be aware that most open-home inspections are timed to coincide with the greatest amount of sunlight entering the home. Typically, all the lights will be turned on as well. It may seem light and bright at 11.00 a.m. when you view it, but at 8.00 a.m. or 3.30 p.m. it could be as dark as a cave. My advice is to arrange to view the home at different times of day, and turn off the lights.

Ask a local

One of the best ways to research a location is to talk to the neighbours. They're probably well versed in the joys and challenges of living in the neighbourhood and have no reason to gild the lily.

It's also prudent to give the neighbours a once-over to make sure they don't have any tastes or habits that will impinge on your enjoyment of your new home. This is especially important for apartment buyers.

A second opinion

It's easy to get attached to a home and, in your enthusiasm, you may overlook certain flaws or issues with the neighbourhood. So I think it's worth getting a member of your family or a friend to accompany you on an inspection to get a second opinion. It can be a sobering experience to have someone point out all the impracticalities and bad points of a home you've fallen in love with. But you're better off having a devil's advocate than making an expensive mistake.

By now you're starting to get to know values, you're going to open inspections, you've established a rapport with agents, and you've started finding a few properties to put on your short list. You're going back at different times of the day, you're researching the area, and you're meeting some neighbours.

You can even ask other agents about properties that you're interested in, just to get another point of view. When I was selling, people would often say to me, 'Have you seen that property Laing & Simmons or L.J. Hooker have got up the road?' I'd be delighted to give them my opinion. If I thought it was be a great property, I wouldn't hesitate to say so.

Of course you've got to be a bit careful, because an agent might overemphasise the negative attributes of the property (after all, they'd prefer you bought the property they're handling). But a good agent who understands relationship-building will most likely be happy to give you a frank and honest opinion about any property in the marketplace.

DUE DILIGENCE

'Due diligence' is an investing term that refers to the process of gathering information with which to evaluate the advantages and risks of a proposed transaction. I strongly recommend you take a businesslike approach when you're buying property and check out all the material facts carefully.

Don't just take the agent's word for anything. You really need to do your own due diligence and make your own assessment of the property's value and condition and the ramifications of the contract of sale.

When it comes to the technical aspects of real estate – such as legal requirements and building inspections – most of us are in the dark. So you'll need some professional help. You have to put your real estate team together, with a solicitor or conveyancer and a pest and building inspector.

THE LAW OF THE LAND

The whole process of buying your home is governed by the contract of sale. Once you've signed the contract, it dictates exactly what you get, when you get it and how much you have to pay. With so much of your money at stake, it's imperative you get legal advice before committing yourself to anything.

The contract of sale must be written and available for viewing before a property is offered for sale. If you're interested in buying the home, get a contract and get it reviewed by your solicitor or conveyancer. Never sign the contract or pay a holding fee without first getting your solicitor or conveyancer to review it for you.

The contract of sale should have the following attachments:

✳ zoning certificate from local council

✳ strata plan if you're buying a unit

✳ sewerage diagram

✳ a copy of the title from the Land Titles Office

✳ documents relating to any easements or restrictive covenants

✳ a cooling-off statement if applicable.

SOLICITOR OR CONVEYANCER?

These days conveyancing is a competitive industry. You can choose between using a solicitor or a conveyancer. Most general practising solicitors are well equipped to do the average property transaction. For anything that's slightly intricate, I would seek the advice of a specialist property lawyer.

The benefit of a conveyancer is that they generally cost less. They don't have the overheads of a solicitor and they do large volumes. The other obvious benefit is that conveyancing is all they do, so they're specialists. They tend to focus on their local area, so they'll have a good relationship with the agents, and they'll know the type of property well.

I don't have a preference for one over the other. If you have a good established relationship with a solicitor, stick with them. Otherwise ask a few people who have bought recently who they used, and if they were happy with the service they received.

REAL ESTATE ROULETTE

Most of us are uninitiated about the technical building aspects of real estate, so I think getting expert advice in those areas is critical. Having worked in real estate for 20 years, I'm always astounded by the small percentage of people who get the proper inspection reports before purchasing. It's certainly less than 20 per cent.

Less than 20 per cent of people get an expert's opinion when buying the most expensive investment of their life! Novices coming into the market and buying property without getting a building report – that's really just asking for it. I mean, what an insurance policy. A building report is like a $500 insurance policy: you get someone to tell you that the house you're buying is not going to fall over.

BUILDING AND PEST INSPECTIONS

A building inspection identifies all necessary repairs, gives you ammunition to negotiate the price with, and allows you to rule out properties with serious defects. To save time and money, it's best to get a building inspector who does pest inspections as well. It's a good idea to tee up a building inspector in advance, because it often takes them a couple of days before they can get to the home.

Ideally you should get someone who is familiar with the area and the housing stock. For example, Victorian terraces are quite different to brand-new homes. I've had building inspectors do reports on Victorian terraces when they've never inspected one before. They've freaked out because they're used to doing new homes. So when they see there's no damp-proof course (protection against rising damp), they knock it on the head and the buyer misses out.

Then the next buyer comes along and gets another building inspector who says, 'Look, you need to know about this, this and this, but this is common in Victorian terraces'. By definition, a building report can unveil a whole range of potential problems. That doesn't necessarily mean you shouldn't buy the place, but at least you buy it with your eyes wide open.

Choosing a building inspector

Just because someone is a builder, plumber, handyman or electrician doesn't mean they're able to make a thorough building inspection report. Make sure you get an experienced, qualified inspector. Check what the inspection will actually cover and make sure they have full professional indemnity and public liability insurance.

No home's perfect

The purpose of a building report is to tell you every single thing that could be wrong. I don't suggest that people look for a perfect scorecard, because they'll never get it. You'll end up never buying anything. As long as you're aware of any defects, how serious they are, how they can be rectified and at what cost, you can make an intelligent assessment to buy or not.

If a house has a defect, it doesn't mean you shouldn't buy it. It just means it's an imperfect house with a defect. Of course you should steer clear of some defects, or you should adjust your offer to reflect the cost of fixing the defect. If there's a substantial amount of building rectification necessary, you might want to drop your offer by $10 000 or $20 000 to allow yourself to do that work.

If you're concerned about potential defects, it's a good idea to meet the inspector at the property after they have completed their inspection. They can show you any significant defects and talk you through the potential problems and costs of rectification. I've seen sales that could have fallen over based on the written report, but I've encouraged the buyer to meet the inspector on site and they've talked through the solution.

What about new homes?

Even if a property is brand new, it's still prudent to get a building inspection. Your building inspector can check for shoddy workmanship, inferior or inappropriate materials having been used, work carried out without council approval, or any defects hidden by the new work.

STRATA REPORT

If you're buying an apartment, someone will need to check the records of the body corporate (known as the owners' corporation in some states). You can do this, or your solicitor or conveyancer can organise it for you.

A pre-purchase inspection of body corporate books should reveal:

✳ the adequacy of book-keeping of the owners' corporation

✳ the amount of money in sinking and administrative funds

✳ any restrictions on the usage of common property

✳ restrictions in the owners' corporation bylaws

✳ disputes between residents

✳ any structural defects or necessary repairs.

Body corporate levies are paid into two funds for running and maintaining the building. The administrative fund covers day-to-day expenses such as insurance, gardening, and electricity and water for the common areas. The sinking fund is for major repairs such as painting the building, replacing the roof or repairing the brickwork.

Be on the lookout for major repairs or maintenance projects that have been mentioned in the minutes of the body corporate meetings. If the body corporate hasn't been budgeting carefully, owners may be required to chip in a lump sum, known as a special levy, for major works. The vendor of an apartment may be selling to avoid such costs.

SURVEY REPORT

If the contract of sale doesn't have a recent survey certificate attached, you may need to get a survey report done. You should check with your lender to see if they require one. If so, your solicitor or conveyancer can help you obtain one. A survey report identifies the property, shows any encroachments onto the property, and whether fences and buildings are within the boundary.

WHAT'S IT WORTH?

'How much should I pay?' is one of the most vexing issues for the home buyer. They must satisfy themselves of the property's value, totally independently of the agent's suggestions.

Always remember, the agent's bill is paid by the vendor. In any negotiation, irrespective of whatever rapport and relationship you've got with the agent, they're representing the vendor's best interests and are being paid to negotiate the highest price on their behalf.

Collating sales data

To help you value a home, you should collate recent sales data. Get details of recent sales in the area from agents, newspapers, local councils and Australian Property Monitors or Residex reports (see below). Have a look at the recently sold homes from the outside to see how they compare to the home you plan to buy.

Remember, no two homes are identical – each has a different condition, renovation and decoration. And no two blocks are exactly the same – they have different sizes, views and positions. So when you're comparing recent sales against the one you want to buy, you'll need to adjust for differences.

The factors to be taken into account include:

✳ the condition of home and garden

✳ location

✳ aspect and views

✳ parking

* renovation potential

* land size

* security.

If you've done your research carefully, you should have a good idea of a home's value. If you're still not sure, you can always pay for an independent valuation.

Online sales data

There are two good online sources of comprehensive recent sales data for home buyers. Australian Property Monitors' *Home Price Guide* (www.homepriceguide.com.au) lists prices of all properties that have sold in a postcode over the previous 12 months. It covers every state except Tasmania. The guide includes both houses and units, and has some details about the property's features.

Residex has a similar report called the *Postcode Explorer* (www.residex.com.au), but it only covers New South Wales, Queensland and Victoria.

Emotional appeal

Do an inventory of all the features of the home you love and the reasons why you'd love to live there. On the other side of the ledger, consider all the downsides of the home, features that you're not so keen on and the money you'll have to spend to make it just right.

When you tally up all the pluses and minuses, you can get a feeling for the emotional appeal of the home. It's the 'how much do you want it?' factor. Now you've got to put a value on this. I'm not necessarily encouraging you to pay over the odds for a home. But if you can afford it and this is the home of your dreams, would you be willing to pay $20 000 more than a home is 'worth' to own it? How about $40 000?

Many buyers add a margin onto their estimated value for the emotional appeal of a home. My recommendation is to consider it before the auction, rather than in the heat of the moment as the hammer is about to fall. Go over your finances and your sales evidence one more time and talk it over with your family.

BUYING BY PRIVATE TREATY

Sale by private treaty (sometimes called 'private sale') is the most common way of selling property in Australia. The home is offered for sale with a set price. Usually the owner sells the property through an agent who markets the property and deals directly with buyers.

The vendor's asking price is not usually the selling price. The asking price is an arbitrary figure that's decided upon by the vendor, usually with some good guidance and comparable sales research by their agent. The selling price is uncovered after a period of negotiation between buyers and the vendor. Offers pass back and forth until the vendor and a buyer come to a meeting of the minds on price.

BUYER BENEFITS

A sale by private treaty is usually less dramatic than an auction. It takes the competitive nature of auction bidding out of the buying process. However, if two buyers have their hearts set on one property, a bidding war can break out, with offers rapidly escalating until one buyer relents. That situation can be every bit as nerve-racking as an auction.

The negotiation process gives buyers time to consider each offer, without the pressure to make a snap decision. At auction, buyers are often tempted to pay a little more than they planned, which might land them in financial difficulties. Thus, buyers usually find it easier to stay within their financial comfort zone with a private treaty sale, especially if the market is hot.

With a private treaty sale, you don't have uncertainty around price. You know you can buy the home for the asking price, and things only get better thereafter if you can negotiate a lower figure.

Private treaty buyers have more room to negotiate terms and conditions which are favourable to them. At auction, all bidding is subject to the contract prepared by the vendor (although the contract can be varied by agreement before the auction). Most states allow a cooling-off period for private treaty sales, so you can back out if you change your mind or find out about any problems with the deal.

It's common practice to get your pest and building inspections done once an offer has been accepted, so you don't have to pay for any reports until you've made an agreement. At auction, the property is sold on the fall of the hammer, so you need to get your inspections done beforehand, even though you may not end up buying the home. If you're the underbidder on several properties, this can add up to a significant expense.

You can still pay a premium

Just because there's no competitive bidding doesn't mean you won't pay a premium with a private treaty. You may well pay over the odds if you don't do your comparable sales research properly.

NEGOTIATION

Negotiating the deal is at the heart of the private treaty process. It's a time-honoured tradition for discovering the market price. However, many of us feel at a loss when it comes to negotiation. Since most Australians buy property so rarely (usually only once every five years or so), very few of us have had enough experience to become skilful negotiators.

Many buyers are uncomfortable with the process, and worried about hurting the vendor's feelings or looking foolish. And while the vendor has the agent to negotiate for them, buyers are at their own mercy. They can get a good deal or they can get done.

All buyers need some negotiation skills, so I've outlined the basic principles for you. Keep in mind that the psychology of negotiation is quite complex: it's not just about getting the best price, but also about creating the perception that your opponent has achieved the best result.

Getting started

Before you begin negotiating, make sure you have your finance pre-approved. You need to be 100 per cent sure you can pay for the home before you make an offer, and you'll only know that by getting your loan pre-approved in writing by your lender. Also, you don't want to risk another buyer coming in and making a better offer while you're arranging finance.

I would also recommend you make sure all the appropriate legal documents are in order before you make an offer. If you have a good relationship with a conveyancer or solicitor, they will often give you some initial free advice on the contracts of properties you're considering buying (on the understanding you'll get them to do the legal work when you buy).

Under no circumstances should you sign a contract of sale before you've had the appropriate legal advice from your solicitor or conveyancer. Unlike an offer, a contract is a legally binding document. If you sign and then don't go through with the sale, you can lose your deposit and be sued for the agreed price.

Know your walk-away price

Before you start making offers, decide where you want to be at the end of the negotiations. Your best outcome is buying the property at or below your walk-away price, with terms you can live with.

Buying real estate, especially if it's your own home, can become an extremely emotionally charged process. Once you fall in love with a home, you've often mentally moved in before you've even agreed on a price.

If your heart takes over from your head and you offer more than you can afford, it can be financially disastrous. The joy of home ownership can easily turn into the nightmare of financial stress if you pay over your financial limit. So you need to be very clear about what price you'll walk away from.

It's a bargain

If you've done your research and found out that the home is priced below the market, don't be afraid to offer full price. If you don't buy it now, someone else will.

Offers and counteroffers

The basic mechanism of negotiation is the counteroffer. The vendor indicates their asking price and interested buyers respond with an initial offer. Buyers often use their first offer to test the waters. Their strategy is to get the vendor to make a counteroffer so they can gauge where their head is at.

If the vendor makes a counteroffer, the negotiations begin in earnest.

When a counteroffer is made, the recipient (the buyer or vendor) has three options:

1. Accept the offer exactly as it is.

2. Reject the offer.

3. Make a counteroffer.

It's important to note that you can't both accept and counter an offer. A counteroffer is a brand-new offer and effectively rejects the previous offer. If, for example, you offer $650 000 with a 12-week settlement, the vendor can't accept the price but demand a 6-week settlement. That amounts to a counteroffer, which you are under no obligation to accept.

The negotiations conclude when an offer is accepted. But there's no legally binding agreement until contracts have been exchanged. That's why it's important to have your lender, building inspector and solicitor or conveyancer standing by so you can act quickly to prevent another buyer making a higher offer before you've exchanged contracts.

I'm serious!

As well as assessing the amount and terms of your offer, the vendor will also want to know how sincere you are about buying their property. Are you a committed home buyer with finance approved, ready to act immediately, or a property investor who's just kicking the tyres to see if they can get a bargain?

You need to communicate to the vendor that you're a serious buyer and you can be trusted. There are several ways to do this. Firstly, make sure you have your finance approved in writing. When you make an offer, the agent will often enquire whether you have finance approval and will relay this information to the vendor. If you make a written offer, make sure you mention that your home loan has been pre-approved.

Putting your offer in writing further demonstrates your commitment. Verbal offers can come and go, but a written offer shows a higher level of commitment. The best way to show you're serious is by signing a contract and attaching a cheque for the deposit. Showing the colour of your money gives you a much better chance of being taken seriously by the vendor.

Attaching a cheque to a signed contract makes your offer a lot more seductive to the vendor. It gives them a great deal of certainty – they can sign the contract and the deal's done. As they say, a bird in the hand ... And it doesn't affect your cash flow because the agent can't bank the cheque until the vendor has exchanged contracts with you. But it makes the offer a lot harder to refuse.

Care, but not that much

One of the best pieces of advice about negotiating I ever got was 'Care, but not that much'. What this means is that it's OK to reveal that you're interested in the property and you'd like to buy it, but don't let on that you're too attached. You've got to give the impression, 'Yeah, I think it's a nice home and I'd like to buy it. But if I don't get it for the right price that's OK, because there are other homes I could buy'.

One way to achieve this state of mind is to genuinely have a few homes on your short list. It's good to keep your options open, because you're in a better bargaining position if you're prepared to walk away. Remember, there's always another home.

If you come across as extremely emotionally attached to the property, you will weaken your negotiating position. If you have an aura of 'I must have it at all costs', the agent will pick up on that and may well advise the vendor to stay firm to see how high you'll go. But if the agent feels that you're in a situation where you're interested in buying the property but you have other options, that's a very strong negotiating position.

Win-win negotiations

I'm a big believer in win-win negotiations. If you can help the vendor get a win, you often get one yourself. I think it's a mistake to be too inflexible. Look for some common ground that works for both parties. Find out what you can do to assist the vendor and give them an incentive to accept your offer. You can often trade off terms favourable to the vendor for a reduction in price.

Be respectful to the vendor

It's not unusual for the process of private treaty negotiation to bring up strong emotions in buyers. If you really love the home, it's hard not to get attached to the outcome of the negotiations. The toing and froing of counteroffers can begin to seem like a battle. Suddenly your ego gets involved, and the process becomes all about winning rather than coming to a mutually agreeable arrangement.

You catch more flies with honey than you do with vinegar, so I think it's important to maintain a good rapport with the other side. You want to maintain a friendly, open and clear relationship with the selling agent, because you won't further your cause by getting into conflict.

It's definitely not in your best interests to offend the vendor, so be careful about anything that you say or put in writing to the agent. There's no point in saying to the agent, 'Look, the reason I'm only prepared to offer this amount is because the décor is disgusting and I'll have to gut the whole house'. It's highly likely that your comment will be communicated to the vendor, they'll get offended and you'll be out of favour.

Vendors are influenced by their emotions too, and people prefer to do business with people they like. Over the years I've had many vendors take a lower offer because they've liked the buyer. I've had people say to me, 'David's such a lovely young man and his fiancée is sweet. It reminds me of what I was like when I bought the place. I know the investor is offering a bit more, but I feel good about going with David'.

Be a straight shooter

Don't play games with the vendor – you'll only antagonise them. If the vendor gets angry with you, the negotiations will break down. They'll either negotiate with another buyer or stand on their price.

NEGOTIATING THE PRICE

Negotiating the price is a time-honoured tradition in private treaty sales, and the asking price is only the starting point for the negotiations. It doesn't necessarily reflect the fair market value of the property. The selling price is invariably lower than the asking price.

Vendors are prepared for a little give-and-take, and they have a perception that your first offer will never be your last. So if you start with your best offer, it's going to be a tough negotiation because you've taken away the vendor's opportunity to negotiate.

It's better to start somewhere below your walk-away price and move your offers upwards in small increments. It's important to keep a couple of concessions up your sleeve, both in your price and your terms.

Avoid making ultimatums such as 'This is my top-dollar price – take it or leave it'. You leave yourself no room to move. If you do make another higher offer, it makes you look untrustworthy. The vendor will immediately think, 'I wonder how high they can go?' When you want to make a new offer, simply say, 'This is my offer'.

The psychology of negotiation

Negotiation is a very psychological process. A skilled negotiator knows how to create and manage perceptions. I find it's not necessarily all about getting the best price – it's about the perception of achieving the best result. When they believe they've achieved the best offer they can get from you, many vendors will accept your offer. It's when they perceive that you've got more in you that they'll tend to sit on their price.

Cheeky offer

If you believe the property is overpriced, you should be prepared to open negotiations with a low or 'cheeky' offer. Just because a property is on the market at $400 000 doesn't mean that's what it's worth. It may ultimately only be worth $350 000. And, to get the negotiations to that point, you might have to start with a low offer.

There's no need to be embarrassed. There's nothing wrong with making a low offer, or asking for favourable terms. However, for a cheeky offer to be effective it needs to be high enough to get the vendor's attention, but low enough to give you room to negotiate up to your walk-away price.

And don't let the agent fob off your low offer – they're bound by law to pass on all legitimate offers to the vendor. However, it's quite a common negotiation strategy to give an instant rejection in an attempt to secure a higher offer.

Some agents will say, 'Look, you're really wasting your time at $420 000. The house is on the market at $480 000, and unless the vendor is very close to that...' If that happens, you have to stand firm and call the agent's bluff. If you've done your research, you should be comfortable with the offer. So you say, 'I totally understand they might reject it, but that's my offer'.

Before you make a cheeky offer, consider how much you really want the home and how upset you'd be if you lost it. If you have your heart set on owning the home, it might be better to start your offers closer to the asking price.

Put it in writing

Agents are obliged to communicate every serious offer to vendors. But in practice this sometimes doesn't happen, especially if your offer is significantly lower than the asking price. If your offer is in writing, it's much less likely to 'disappear'.

Don't play it too cool

Over the years there have been many times where I've been negotiating with a buyer and they've told me they're at their limit, they won't make another offer, they're looking at other properties and they've made offers elsewhere. So I've taken them at their word and sold the property to someone else.

But then they come back to me and they're irate. They say, 'I would have bought it – I would have paid more!' So you have to be a little bit careful that you don't play it too cool and negotiate yourself out of a purchase. You can't blame the agent if you show lack of interest and claim you're at your limit, and they go and sell it to another party. It's a fine line between not appearing too keen and appearing uninterested.

Odd amounts

I've often successfully made offers at odd amounts, especially after I've already made a couple of lower offers. For example, rather than offering $460000 or $465000, I'll offer $463500. I'll tell the agent, 'I've looked at the comparable sales, and I've looked at my finances and costs, and I can offer $463500'. An odd amount suggests that there's some science and logic to your offer – that you're basing it on some objective criteria. It also implies that you're at your financial limit and have no more to spend.

NEGOTIATING TERMS AND CONDITIONS

There's an old saying in negotiation: 'If you can't get your price, get your conditions'.

But many buyers get so fixated on getting the lowest price that they forget there are other aspects of the deal they can negotiate on. The terms and conditions of the contract can be powerful bargaining chips. Using them as trade-offs is a flexible way to add value to the deal without paying any more cash.

You may be able to stand firm on your price, but give the vendor favourable terms to sweeten the deal. For example, the vendors might want to stay in the home until after Christmas. You might be able to get them to agree to your price if you give them a longer settlement, allowing them to stay in the home for a few extra months.

It's all about finding out what the vendors want and giving it to them, while still getting what you want. Consider negotiating on the following terms.

Settlement

The standard settlement period is six weeks. But vendors are often working to a short timetable, so if you can offer them a quick settlement they may be more willing to accept your offer. On the other hand, some vendors may want to stay in their home until they've bought another property, so offer them an extended settlement.

Inclusions

If the vendor won't budge on price, perhaps there's something in the home that they'll include to sweeten the deal. Did you like the look of that rug in the living room?

Releasing the deposit

Often the vendor is out there trying to secure another property. If you release your deposit so the vendor can use it as a deposit on their new home, they might be tempted to run with your offer. But you should always seek your solicitor's or conveyancer's advice before you agree to release your deposit.

Occupancy

If the property is vacant, the owner may be willing to give you early occupancy in return for rent. Or, for a period after the sale, you might allow the vendor to stay in the property for an agreed rent.

Repairs

You can make a higher offer contingent on the vendor undertaking certain repairs on the property.

My top six negotiation tips

1. Care, but not that much.

2. Always be respectful to the vendor – it's not personal.

3. Get time on your side – give your offers a deadline.

4. Find out the vendor's motivation – a vendor in a jam will give you a better deal.

5. Win-win negotiations are best – be willing to give a little.

6. If you can't get your price, get your conditions.

KNOWLEDGE IS POWER

One of the keys to being a successful negotiator is acquiring knowledge, both about negotiating in general and the vendor's circumstances in particular. The more information you have – about the state of the market, the motivation of the vendor and the condition of the house – the better position you're in to negotiate.

The challenge is that most of the information you'd like to know – such as why the vendor is selling and what's their walk-away price – is not easy to find out. Agents are trained not to divulge any information that could prejudice the sale, but of course sometimes they do slip up. You can also glean a lot of information from reading between the lines.

If you find out the vendor's reason for selling, you might discover how determined they are to get a particular price. Perhaps they have to finance a home they've already bought. Do they have a sell-by date? Perhaps they'd be amenable to a quick settlement.

Find out how long the home has been on the market. If the property has been for sale for a long time, it could mean several things. The vendors might be refusing to budge from an inflated price, or maybe there's something wrong with the property that you haven't noticed. But, if the vendors are feeling frustrated because they realise they got the pricing wrong, they may be keen to sell.

What's their motivation?

Possibly the most valuable information is the vendor's motivation for selling. If you can get an understanding of where they're at, and what their next move is, you can figure out how you might be able to assist them, and get a good deal as well.

Time is a factor. The longer you can draw out the process, the more likely you are to find out about the vendor's motivation. But beware you don't wait too long, or someone else might buy the property.

When you're inspecting the property, make sure you quiz the agent about information that will help you in the negotiation stage. The agent might not tell you, but it can't hurt to ask the following questions:

* How long has the home been listed for?

* Why are the owners selling?

* How did you work out the price?

* If the property has been passed in at auction, how much was the highest bid?

* When do the owners want to move out?

Justify your offer

You have to try to take your emotions out of the equation at the point of negotiation. You can't change how you feel about the property, or how much you want to own it. But you have to sit down and decide your price, based on the objective factors of comparable sales and other current options.

Once you've made your assessment of price, it's a good strategy to justify your offer with factual information. Give the agent details of recent comparable sales and other comparable properties that are on the market that are influencing the price you're offering.

However, I would advise against cataloguing all the faults and shortcomings of the home. There are no perfect properties; every property has its flaws and imperfections. It's all part of the deal, and they've probably been assessed by the vendor and the agent when they initially priced the property.

However, even if you've agreed on a price, if the pest and building reports come back with some problems, rather than pulling out of the sale, you can renegotiate the price. The vendor may or may not go along, but don't think that once you've agreed on a price (but haven't exchanged contracts) that the opportunity to change that based on new information is gone.

Valuation = ammunition

A valuation from a licensed appraiser that is much lower than the asking price can provide good ammunition to shift a vendor's price down.

Deadlines on offers

When you communicate your offer – whether in writing or verbally – it's a good idea to put a deadline on it. You want to give the vendor enough time to contemplate the offer, but you don't want to leave it open-ended. A deadline encourages the vendor to make a decision.

A deadline by the close of business the day following the offer is enough time. The vendor can sleep on it and discuss it with all the decision-makers. The longer the vendor takes to make a decision, the bigger chance there is of a higher offer coming in. Also, the agent can use your offer to encourage other buyers to go higher.

People will usually take as long as you give them to make a decision. So if you say, 'This offer is good for 72 hours', the vendor will probably take 72 hours to decide. If the vendor hasn't made a decision by your deadline, just extend the deadline. You don't have to change your price or terms.

WINNING TACTICS

Winning at poker is rarely about the best hand – it's more about the mental game. Real estate negotiation is the same. The key factors are: coming from a position of strength; creating immediacy, and not being too attached to the outcome.

Being well researched puts you in a position of strength, as the person with the most information usually has the upper hand. Making an unconditional offer on a signed contract with a deposit cheque and a deadline creates immediacy and prompts the vendor to act now. And caring, but not that much, enables you to maintain a poker face – but that's not easy when you're looking at your potential future home.

A helping hand

Very few people have bought enough property to become skilful negotiators. I hope my tips and hints will help you feel more confident and enable you to secure a good deal. But if you're still feeling a little anxious about your ability to get the best price, I recommend you seriously consider getting someone to help you.

A third party can be more objective, and they're less likely to be affected by emotions. Solicitors and accountants can be of assistance because quite often they are experienced negotiators (check first though). If you have a good relationship with a real estate agent (who's not connected to this particular sale), they too can be an ally in this situation.

Buyers' agents can also be an asset to your team. They are licensed real estate agents who help buyers find and buy property. They are usually expert negotiators and, for a small fee, will negotiate a favourable purchase price and conditions for you.

Buyers' agents are invaluable if you're a novice property buyer or have little time to home hunt. As well as negotiating deals, they can research the market and find a property that meets your requirements and budget, and even arrange your finance and recommend a conveyancer. It's a very big business in America, where lots of buyers use them, and it's starting to take off here.

GAZUMPING

Gazumping is when your offer has been accepted by the vendor, but before you've exchanged contracts, they sell the property to someone else without giving you the opportunity to increase your offer. It's a terrible letdown for buyers, who are usually left feeling angry and betrayed.

Unfortunately gazumping is a fact of life. You can't rely on a 'gentlemen's agreement' in real estate. Buyers have to accept that nothing is certain until contracts have been exchanged. A letter of offer is not binding on either party — there's no binding sale until you have a signed contract of sale from the vendor.

What sometimes happens is that buyers get a verbal acceptance of their offer and then they relax. 'OK, all the hard work's done', they think to themselves. 'We'll get the contract to our solicitor, get the bank to do the valuation next week, and in a couple of weeks we'll exchange.'

But you can't relax, because the time from your offer being accepted to the exchange of contracts is the danger period. There's nothing to stop other offers being made, and the agent is obligated by law to refer any further offers to the vendor.

A buyer who saw the property two weeks ago but has been overseas on business could ring up the agent only to find out an offer has been accepted. Not to be outdone, she says, 'Well, I'll pay full price. I'd like you to communicate my offer to the vendor'. Whether the agent likes that situation or not, they are obliged to forward the offer. Then it's the vendor's decision.

Take precautions

Gazumping only really takes place in the event that there is a delay between an offer being accepted and exchanging contracts. So it's imperative to minimise that time period. Have your finance pre-approved, your building inspector on stand-by, and get your solicitor or conveyancer to look at the contract before you make an offer.

Be careful about bluffing about your walk-away price too, because that can really backfire on you. You can't blame the agent for believing you when you said you couldn't pay any more. If you're really concerned about being gazumped, you can offer the asking price (although that's no guarantee – someone might still offer more).

If the agent does come back to you after you've agreed on price and says a last minute higher offer has been made, you need to assess your options carefully. Find out what the vendor will agree to. For example, if you match the new offer will they go with you, or do you have to make another higher offer? Beware of getting caught in a Dutch auction. You can always walk away if you want to.

Eager third party

When you're negotiating, it's not uncommon for the agent to tell you about other parties who are interested in buying the property. The 'eager third party' is quite a common negotiation tactic. You need to be aware that in some cases there may not be another buyer. Unethical? Sure, but it's a reality. So you need to keep your wits about you, use your intuition and be prepared to walk away if you feel you're being conned.

SUBJECT-TO OFFERS

You can make your offer contingent on certain conditions, such as your finance being approved, getting a favourable valuation on the property or a clean bill of health from the pest and building inspector. These 'subject-to' clauses give you an opportunity to back out of the sale if certain conditions aren't met.

However, you'll find that vendors and agents don't look favourably at subject-to offers. If a vendor agrees to a subject-to contract, they are tied up, but the buyer has a way out. The vendor can't accept a higher offer if one comes along, but the buyer can pull out if their conditions aren't met, leaving the buyer high and dry.

Subject-to offers are a bit of a dying art. These days buyers can get their finance approved and inspection reports done in a day or two. So vendors are happy to agree on a price, but won't lock themselves out of the opportunity to take someone else's higher offer until you sign an unconditional contract.

BUYING OFF THE PLAN

The essence of property is that it's a 'real' asset. It's a tangible asset made up of soil, bricks and mortar. The exception to this concept is buying off the plan, where a developer offers an apartment or house for sale before the building has been completed.

Buying off the plan has been popular on the Gold Coast for many years, and it's rapidly catching on in the rest of Australia. The reason that many developers sell off the plan is so they can secure finance upfront. Often a lender won't provide funds until the developer has exchanged a certain number of contracts on a proposed apartment block.

Advantages and risks

The advantages for buyers are that developers often sell off the plan at a discount, and the extended settlement gives you time to sell your existing property and get the best loan deal. Also, if the market is rising, you can make a capital gain with little outlay. Typically, the building construction period for many developments is 18 months and up to three years, and you're securing the home with a deposit.

The property is valued at today's dollars. So, in a rising market, people who buy an apartment off the plan for $400 000 may find that it's worth $480 000 when they settle two years later. They've made a capital gain before they've even moved in.

Of course, the opposite is also true. The property market may fall, and your home will be worth less when it's completed than when you bought it. Or, by the time you move in, there may be an oversupply of apartments, diluting the market and depressing prices.

Off-the-plan pitfalls

There are all sorts of things that can go wrong between signing the contract and moving in:

* delays in completion – you may have to wait much longer to move in than you anticipated

* the home might turn out to be different than you imagined

* interest rates could rise before you settle

* the builder and/or developer could go bust before you settle – you may have to shell out more money to get your home finished

* the quality of construction and finishes might be less than you'd hoped for.

Bigger is not necessarily better

Buying off the plan is definitely a science in itself. When you're selecting an apartment, you need to be able to interpret the floor plan. Developers usually price apartments based on a square metre rate. There are different rates for different views, aspects and locations. But, generally speaking, apartments that are grouped close together will have a similar square metre rate.

When you're comparing two apartments, you need to look beyond the price and size and assess which has the best floor plan. A 60-square-metre apartment might be a better buy than a 70-square-metre apartment two doors down if the smaller apartment has a more livable layout and no wasted space.

From an investor's point of view, the two apartments would probably get the same rent, so the smaller one has a better return on investment. And if they were to be sold in five years, they'd probably go for roughly the same price, even though the larger one was initially sold for 15 per cent more.

Make sure you carry out the following checks before you sign on the dotted line:

1. Check out the display unit in detail.

2. Review the contract carefully, especially with regard to:

    ✳ finishes and fittings – are substitutions permitted?

    ✳ can the apartment be on sold before completion?

    ✳ completion date delays – do you have any 'get out' clauses if it's not finished on time?

    ✳ defects identified post-completion – will the builder rectify any?

3. Check the layout of the building from the plans – where is your apartment in relation to views, common areas and lifts?

4. Visit the site and check the location and aspect.

5. Check out other developments the builder and developer have done - inspect them if possible, and talk to the strata manager about any problems with the building.

Forewarned is forearmed

I'm not trying to scare you away from buying off the plan. But it is inherently more risky than buying established property, so you really need to keep your wits about you.

BUYING AT AUCTION

An auction is an exciting way to buy property. It condenses the entire negotiation process into a half-hour or so. All the elements of a negotiation meet at one point in time, and you're often standing at the property of your dreams trying to outbid several other buyers. It can get highly emotional.

There are hundreds of auctions across the country almost every weekend of the year. And, just as each property has a unique combination of features, each auction has a different energy. Each auctioneer has their own style, and the crowd reaction can range from total lack of interest to buyer frenzy. You never know how many bidders there will be, or their level of interest.

Because most people don't bid at auction very often in their lives, they're usually very unsure about how the game is played. Confidence is a key component of buying at auctions, and knowledge helps build confidence. So, to help demystify the process, I'll explain how auctions work and give you some of my best bidding strategies.

AUCTION BASICS

An auction is a public sale by a licensed auctioneer where the property is sold to the highest bidder. The vendor puts a reserve price on the property and it will not be sold until bidding has exceeded this price. If the bidding doesn't reach the reserve price, the property is passed in and the highest bidder usually has the first right to negotiate with the vendor.

Auctions are held on site or in the agent's auction rooms. Before the auction begins, the vendor will set a reserve price in consultation with their agent. The reserve price is not revealed to bidders before the auction. The auctioneer opens the proceedings by giving an overview of the home's features. If the auction is in auction rooms, there may also be a brief slideshow on the property.

Bidding usually starts at a modest level and proceeds upwards until the reserve price is reached. At this point the auctioneer usually calls the property on the market by saying 'The property is now on the market' or 'I can sell'. The property is sold to the highest bidder and contracts are signed and exchanged immediately.

If the bidding stalls before the reserve price is met, there are several ways the auction can go. The agent will liaise with the vendor and determine if they wish to lower their reserve to the current bid. If this happens, the bidding might continue, or, if not, the home is sold at the current bid. Alternatively, if the vendor declines to lower the reserve, the property is passed in. The highest bidder then has an opportunity to negotiate a price with the vendor.

Public negotiation

The reason why auctions are successful for buyers and sellers is immediacy. A buyer knows if they put their hand in the air right now they can probably own it. And a seller knows if they accept the highest bid that they've sold it. It works really well for both parties. An auction is really just a public negotiation. You've got a vendor on one side of the table and multiple buyers on the other. Everyone's discussing price and, by the end of the auction, the best offer will come forward and the vendor will say 'yes' or 'no'.

BUYER BENEFITS

I'm a fan of buying property at auction. Almost of all of the properties I have bought for myself have been at auction. Even with my experience as a real estate agent and auctioneer, I find them quite stressful, but I like the immediacy of the process. I also like being able to assess my competition on the day and observe them bidding, as opposed to private treaty negotiation, which takes place behind closed doors.

Through competitive bidding, an auction establishes a security price benchmark for buyers. In private treaty negotiations, you have no idea what competing buyers are prepared to offer. You can place an offer of $650 000, because that's what your research indicates is a fair price. But you don't know if the next highest offer was $600 000, $649 000 or $550 000.

At auction, if someone bids $680 000, then I bid $682 000, and another bidder comes in at $683 000, we're all on the same page in terms of value. When a property is knocked down to you, you know someone else is willing to pay about the same amount you were. So there's a high degree of comfort that the price is right, because it's been benchmarked in public.

And while it's true that in-demand property can get a premium price at auction, it's also true that you can pick up a bargain at an auction. In fact, you'll find some of the best buys come from auctions. If a vendor is committed to selling on the day, they might be disappointed with the highest bid, but they'll often make the decision to sell anyway.

Top four auction benefits

1.   The price is benchmarked with other buyers in public – this is the market talking.

2.   You get an immediate result.

3.   If you're the winning bidder, you won't be gazumped.

4.   You can pick up a bargain.

AUCTION ANXIETY

Not everyone shares my enthusiasm for buying property at auction. In fact, less than 5 per cent of buyers in Australia nominate auction as their preferred method of buying property. Many people are intimidated by the process and are wary of getting caught up in the emotion on the day and paying too much.

I totally understand how people get nervous at auctions. Even after all my years as an agent and auctioneer, I still feel the surge of adrenaline when I'm bidding on a home. But, if you avoid auctions because you're uncomfortable with the process, you're going to miss a lot of good buying opportunities, because most of the better properties around Australia are now sold by auction (especially in Sydney and Melbourne).

What you need is a strategy to overcome your fear. I always recommend attending a few auctions before you actually bid on a home. You'll get more comfortable with the setting and atmosphere, the auctioneer's patter and the pace and tension of the event. You'll see which bidding strategies work and which don't.

Get someone to bid for you

If you're still anxious about bidding at auction, you can always get someone to bid on your behalf. I've often gone to auctions on behalf of friends and clients. Someone who is experienced and familiar with the auction scenario won't be intimidated by the auctioneer or the process, and is definitely a good ally to have.

If you don't have any friends or relatives with suitable experience, you can always get a buyers' agent to bid for you. They're well aware of all the auction tricks and traps. And, while there's no guarantee you'll win the auction, it's much easier for someone who's an experienced bidder and not emotionally attached to the sale to project confidence. Plus, they won't get carried away and go over your limit.

Don't tell the agent your top price

It's in your interest to keep your walk-away price a secret from the agent. If they find out how high you can go, they'll use that information to help the vendors to set their reserve.

BUYING BEFORE AUCTION

A lot of buyers don't realise you can buy a property before the auction. This is another good strategy if you're not confident bidding at auction. Simply ask the agent if the vendor is willing to sell privately. If your offer is right, the vendor may be willing to sell before auction. Our company sells 25 to 30 per cent of our auction listings prior to auction day.

If the market is rising or hot, it's in your advantage to try to secure the property without the competition of others. Whether the vendor will accept your offer depends a lot on market conditions. If buyer interest is poor, a vendor may be more open to a pre-auction offer. However, if the market is hot the vendor is more likely to let the price be determined by competitive bidding.

Some vendors will be inclined to sell before auction if you offer them what they consider to be a premium price, or if you're the only interested buyer. If you've done your research and you'd like to secure the property before auction, I recommend offering close to your walk-away price. You'll also need to waive your right to cooling off to show the vendor you're a serious buyer.

Of course, one of the risks of making a pre-auction offer is that you've shown your hand. You've given the vendor a line in the sand to set the reserve. If other bidders aren't prepared to go that high, the vendor can put in a bid just below the reserve. After all, if you were prepared to pay that amount before auction, why wouldn't you pay it now?

Your pre-auction offer can be used to lever other buyers up to a higher price. You could find yourself in a bidding war before the auction has even begun. Ethical agents won't entertain these tactics, but you need to be aware that sometimes it goes on.

Negotiating terms and conditions

A sale at auction is subject to the contract of sale (you can get a copy from the agent). If you want to vary the terms (e.g. from a 6-week settlement to 12 weeks), feel free to ask the agent if the vendor will agree to that. But always get confirmation in writing, before the auction, that those terms will be varied if you're the successful bidder.

THE BID IS WITH WHO?

The vendor is usually legally entitled to bid on their own property at auction. This is known as 'vendor bidding'. The purpose is to help the property reach its reserve price. A vendor bid is typically used to start the auction off, or to bring the bidding closer to the reserve if it stalls. If there are no bidders, the auctioneer will sometimes pass in the property on a vendor bid.

You should be aware that perhaps not every bid you see made on a property at an auction is necessarily from a genuinely interested buyer. The bid may be from a representative of the vendor. The laws and codes of practice relating to vendor bidding vary from state to state.

The vendor may be limited in the number of bids they can make, and the auctioneer may have to announce when a vendor bid is made and by whom. In New South Wales, for example, the auctioneer has the right to make one bid on behalf of the vendor, which must be disclosed at the time of making such a bid. Vendor bids can only be made up to the reserve price.

Laws of the land

Every state in Australia has different rules for auctions, so it's worthwhile doing a little bit of research on your rights and responsibilities. Pay particular attention to the regulations on vendor bidding and the rights of the highest bidder. Contact the Real Estate Institute or the fair trading/consumer affairs office in your state.

Before you buy a home at auction, you should check your local legislation to see if the vendor has the right to make any bids and whether they must be disclosed. If you're in any doubt about whether vendor bids can be made, you can ask the auctioneer on the day if the vendor is intending to make any bids during the auction. By asking in the public forum, you're a putting a greater obligation on the auctioneer to adhere to whatever they tell you.

Auction transparency

I applaud the recent legislation aimed at regulating vendor bidding and making the auction process more transparent. Anything that gives buyers more confidence is a good thing for the real estate industry.

But when people talk about lack of transparency in auctions, I think you have to compare them to the alternative, which is negotiation by private treaty. Unfortunately, private treaty also offers unscrupulous agents opportunities to mislead and deceive buyers.

Phantom offers from nonexistent private treaty buyers are not unknown. If you make an offer and the agent tells you there are other buyers who are willing to offer more, how can you tell if they're genuine or not? Where's the transparency there? In most instances, I'd rather be able to see my competing buyers and make my own assessment as to their bona fides.

Be prepared

If you're the highest bidder when the hammer falls, you're legally bound to buy the home, even if there's a structural defect, an onerous condition in the contract or your lender refuses your finance. So it's imperative to have all your due diligence complete and funds ready to pay the deposit before auction day.

Start low

Unfortunately there's no bidding strategy with guaranteed success, except having the most money to spend! Some bidders try an early, high 'knockout' bid in an attempt to scare off more timid bidders. Other bidders wait until the last moment to make their first bid. It's a good idea to attend a few auctions as an observer to see different bidding strategies in action.

One of my tactics is to make a low bid to start the auction. At the outset, you don't know how many interested parties there are (if any), and how much they're prepared to bid. So there's no need to put in a high bid in the early stages. Just place a low bid and see where the auction goes from there.

If you open the auction with a low bid, the auctioneer will note your interest. They'll keep their eye on you so you're less likely to be missed when the bidding heats up. Once the bidding starts, just sit tight, size up the other bidders and watch how the auction unfolds.

Unless the property looks like it's going to be passed in, I won't bid again until the reserve price has been met. When the home has been called on the market, the property is truly for sale. There are no more vendor bids and every bidder is playing for keeps.

Project confidence

The one auction strategy that I have observed working consistently is creating the impression that you will continue to bid until you own the home, no matter what. It's about projecting confidence and psyching out the other bidders. More timid bidders are often put off by an aura of unstoppable self-assurance, and they'll stop bidding.

You must create the perception that you don't have a limit. On a few occasions after I've had a property knocked down to me, I've overheard other bidders saying, 'He would have kept going until he bought it'. In fact, I may have been down to my last bid, but it's obviously in my interest to appear as though I will keep bidding.

I wait until near the end of the auction, when the bidding has slowed down and the other bidders are starting to lose steam. The auctioneer will start the 'going once, going twice ...' routine, and then I'll come in with a clear and confident bid. If the other buyers make further bids, I immediately respond with a higher bid.

Assertive bidding

My bids are fast and assertive. Agonising over every bid is a definite sign of weakness. If a buyer is looking worried and having hushed conversations with their partner every time they make a bid, that's a clear signal they're near (or over) their limit. You don't want to send this signal to other bidders, because they know if they keep going a little bit longer they've got you.

So you have to keep your cool, even if you're only a few thousand from your limit. Don't hesitate on your bids. If other buyers are dithering over their bids, you can knock the wind out of their sails by immediately responding with a higher bid. Be prepared to bid confidently up to your limit and then walk away.

Rather than nodding your head or holding up your paddle to agree to the auctioneer's suggested bid, I recommend calling out the amount of the bid in full. This allows you to project confidence and determination with your tone of voice. It also reinforces the full price being bid, rather than the increment, which may be only $5000, $1000 or even $500.

When the bidding is down to small increments, it's easy for buyers to lose sight of the amount of money being bid. Calling out the full amount of your bid is a reality check for other buyers, who may be at or above their limit. A few extra $1000 bids may not seem like much. But if you call out 'four hundred and seventy-two thousand', your competition might suddenly realise they're actually $7000 over their limit and stop bidding.

If the property is passed in

If the property is passed in, it's a big advantage to be the highest bidder. The highest bidder is usually given the first opportunity to negotiate to buy the property. (Whether this is a legal right or merely a traditional courtesy differs from state to state.) In my experience, well over 50 per cent of passed-in auctions sell to the highest bidder. So you want to put yourself in the box seat to negotiate with the vendor.

The bidding strategy is essentially the same as above. However, you need to pay close attention to vendor bidding. If you're the only interested buyer, you don't want to bid the price up against the vendor, because essentially you're bidding against yourself. But if there are other interested parties, you want to manoeuvre yourself into the position of highest bidder.

However, if you're not the highest bidder, but you're still interested in buying the property, you should definitely let the agent know. You're still in with a chance to buy the property if negotiations break down with the highest bidder, or if you're prepared to pay more than they are.

Stick to your walk-away price

The rapid pace of an auction leaves you little time to make decisions on the fly. With a private treaty sale, you have the opportunity to rethink your position on price with every counter offer. You can talk your offer over with your partner, redo your sums and, literally, sleep on it.

At an auction, you don't have this luxury. You may well be put in a position where you have to make a snap decision about something that can have long-term repercussions for your life. Do you go $10000 over the limit you've set in your head, or risk missing out on a home that could bring you much happiness and security for years to come?

Rather than putting yourself in a position where you have to make these decisions on the spot, it's advisable to think through all the angles before auction day. Know your walk-away price – you have to go into an auction knowing at what figure you absolutely will not make another bid.

An auction is a highly emotionally charged event. But, despite your strong feelings, you don't have to 'win' at all costs. You only win an auction if you buy the property at your price. It's better to feel the short-lived disappointment of missing out on a property you love than the long-lasting remorse of paying too much and putting yourself in financial hardship.

The hand of fate

At an auction, the person who wants it the most and has the biggest chequebook will buy the home. So you need to be mentally prepared to miss out, because you could be outbid. Having a slightly fatalistic approach can help. Go hard for what you're after, but in the back of your mind accept that if circumstances continue to mount up to prevent you from owning a home, there's a message in it and there are always other options.

I've auctioned thousands of properties over the years, and invariably the first conversations I have when I get back to my office after an auction are not with the buyer, who's probably off celebrating with a bottle of champagne, but with the underbidder. The underbidder is usually feeling very dejected, so I try to reassure them that they will find something else that's as good, if not better.

And in almost every instance, when the underbidder later buys another home they say to me, 'You know, you were right. A month ago I didn't believe we'd find a better place. I appreciated you saying it, but I didn't believe it. But I reckon this place is better than the one I missed out on'. Experience has told me that fate plays a hand in finding the right home, and you should go with it.

But it's a fine line. I don't think you should be too casual, because otherwise you'll never get into the market. You have to set your sights, create an action plan and go hard. But also accept that if it's not meant to be, it's not meant to be. Be assured, though, that you can always find the perfect home in your price range sooner or later (hopefully sooner!).

SELLING

CHOOSING THE BEST AGENT

C hoosing the best agent to sell your property is the second most important decision in real estate (after choosing the right property to buy). But from my experience many people are too casual in their approach to this crucial decision. They ring a couple of agents and choose the one who gives them the highest valuation or has the lowest commission.

In my opinion that's the wrong way to choose an agent. There's a lot at stake, so it's worthwhile putting some time and effort into researching your choices. Because choosing a mediocre agent who offers a cheap commission or gives you an inflated valuation of your property is a mistake that can leave you seriously out of pocket.

Speak to your friends and colleagues, browse a few real estate websites, visit some open-home inspections and attend a couple of auctions. Create a series of questions that you want to ask agents, and interview a few as if you're considering them for a job.

MONEY IN YOUR POCKET

I'm sure you've heard about (or seen on television) an auction where competitive bidding ended in a sale price tens of thousands of dollars above the reserve price. You might think the seller just got lucky – that the price was achieved simply because that property was highly sought after or the market was extremely buoyant.

That may well be the case. But it's more likely that the result was the culmination of a few weeks' hard work by a skilful agent. You can reverse-engineer from the auction to see what actions the agent took to create the best possible conditions for that competitive bidding to occur.

The agent probably started by recommending a high-quality marketing plan. They probably did a great job of writing the ad and getting the photographs taken. The marketing plan probably included online elements, such as listings on the agent's website and real estate portals, which have sophisticated search features and e-mail property alerts for buyers.

The agent may have recommended a listing in their in-house magazine that is distributed to buyers at open homes and from their office. The agent would have matched buyers from their database and introduced them to the property. They probably helped the owner present the home in its best light by offering some good recommendations on presentation and styling.

They've almost certainly done a great job in responding to all buyer enquiries to ensure that every potential buyer was followed up and given the opportunity to get excited about the property. The agent has formulated a good auction strategy and briefed an expert auctioneer who's experienced at getting top prices from bidders.

When you break it down, you can see where the extra money comes from. It hasn't just materialised out of thin air. The premium price is the net result of the agent's skill, effort and experience.

I have said to many vendors, 'You're not hiring me to sell your property, because you could do that yourself. You can put an ad in the *Sydney Morning Herald* this week. Spruce up your home on Friday afternoon, make it easy to inspect, and if the price is about right you'll sell it'. What they hire *me* for is the extra 10 per cent that I can extract from the market.

AGENT'S SKILL SET

When you choose an agent, the most important criterion is their ability to maximise the sale price. The skill set that you're looking for includes creative and targeted marketing, outstanding auction strategy and auctioneering skills, superior negotiation skills, and the ability to get into the hearts and minds of buyers, and get them excited about owning your property.

The agent must be capable of marketing the property to the maximum number of buyers. Because the number of buyers you introduce to a property has a direct relationship with the sale price. They must be able to sell the benefits of your property and clearly articulate its advantages over others in the market.

A good agent has credibility and a solid reputation in the community, so when they say something, buyers listen and believe it. They can put together an effective auction strategy and conduct a successful auction. If you're selling by private treaty, you're hiring the agent for their negotiation skills. I believe a good agent can gain an extra 10 to 15 per cent in the negotiation phase alone.

FINANCIAL BENEFITS

The difference between an unskilled agent and a very good agent could easily amount to a 25 to 30 per cent difference on the sale price. The difference between choosing a mediocre agent and the best agent in your area could easily amount to an extra $40 000 or more in your pocket. Now, let's think about that $40 000 for a moment.

If you've just sold your own home, there's no capital gains tax, so the $40 000 extra your agent has extracted from the market is a tax-free bonus. For the average Australian, to earn $40 000 after tax means earning around $80 000 before tax – that amounts to roughly two years' work. So the financial benefit of choosing a good agent to sell your home could be the financial equivalent of two years' income.

I hope I've convinced you of the value of taking the time to do some research to find the best agent to sell your home. With so much of your money at stake, it's a really critical decision, so don't be too casual about whom you appoint to sell your property.

Trust issues

always say to my agents that people don't give their best friends the keys to their house, but they give them to their agent. There's a huge degree of trust required in the agent–vendor relationship, and for this reason alone you should choose your agent carefully.

Short-listing agents

The first step in the research process is drawing up a short list of agents to interview. It's a good idea to talk to at least three agents. As with all professional service providers, I always recommend you begin your search with third-party referrals. Ask around your workplace, your friends and family. Who have they used lately and what was their experience?

Even if your friends and colleagues haven't sold a home recently, they may have been home hunting or bought a home recently. If so, find out which agents impressed them. Who followed them up and was working hard for the vendor to ensure a premium price was achieved? Which agents did they find trustworthy and offered good advice?

Many vendors attend a few open-home inspections in their neighbourhood before they list their homes, so they can see what's on the market and get a feel for the prices being achieved. This is also an excellent way to audition agents to sell your home. You can actually see the agents in action. How they treat you is how they'll treat buyers when they inspect your home.

Finally, you should investigate who the dominant agents are in your area. Take a walk or a drive around your suburb and see who has the most 'sold' signs. Signboards are a highly visible indicator of an agent's market share. Also, have a look in your local paper and see who has the lion's share of the property advertising pages.

If 40 per cent of the vendors in your area have chosen a particular agent, it will be worthwhile seeing what they can do for you. An agent with a large market share is likely to have significant back-office resources, which can also be to your advantage. However, I would recommend interviewing a smaller agent too – someone who is fairly boutique, perhaps a niche player. It never hurts to canvass a variety of different opinions.

Interviewing agents

When you're interviewing agents, you're looking for the best person to sell your home. You want to see what skills and talents they have to offer and whether there's enough rapport for you to be able to work well together. But it's also an opportunity to find out about the state of the market and compare different opinions and approaches to the sales process.

When I've been interviewed by vendors, there are generally half a dozen key questions they're keen to ask:

* What do you think my property is worth?

* How can I maximise the sale price?

* What's the best method of selling my property?

* What's an approximate time frame?

* What's it going to cost me?

* Why should I hire you?

With regard to what your home's worth, clearly you want to go with an agent who is basing their estimated sale price on tangible facts – recent sales data. I'd be concerned if a vendor said, 'Well, I want a million', and the agent replied, 'Oh, that sounds about right'. You have to be wary of agents just telling you what they think you want to hear.

A more switched-on agent would say something like, 'Well, I think a million's achievable and let me show you why. These last four properties in your neighbourhood have sold between $950 000 and $1 050 000 and let me show you how they were comparable to your home …'

Or they might say, 'Tell me a little bit more about your valuation, because the comparable research that I've done puts similar properties in the neighbourhood at around $900 000 to $925 000. So I'm really open to getting a premium price, because that's what I'm paid for. But at this point I really want to get a sense of how you've come up with your figure'.

In some instances you really need the agent to challenge you and educate you to the realities of the current market. Because your hopeful price may not be realistic, and that could lead to problems selling the house. Some of the best homes in the world remain unsold due to an unrealistic price.

Buying the listing

Don't fall into the trap of selecting your agent of the basis of who gives the highest valuation. Some agents will inflate their appraisal in the hope of winning your business. It's known as 'buying the listing'. Once you've hired them, they'll start trying to convince you to accept less than their valuation price.

Presentation

When the conversation turns to maximising the sale price, a lot of agents are less than honest. Perhaps out of a fear of insulting the vendor and losing their business, many agents won't tell the vendor that the property needs some TLC to maximise its sale potential. They just say, 'Oh, this house is just perfect – I wouldn't do a thing'.

I would be a bit sceptical of an agent who defaults to the easiest answer. You really want an agent who is totally honest with you and who is prepared to say, 'I think the home presents well, but there are three or four things I would do to take it to the next level so we can get that premium price I spoke about'.

Often the vendor already knows what needs to be done. They know there are a few spots on the carpet that need to be removed, a few knobs that need replacing in the kitchen, the kids' bedrooms could use a coat of paint and the garden needs pruning. When the agent doesn't speak up, they lose credibility right away.

It's really critical that the agent is not only totally frank and honest with you, but also knowledgeable about the best way to present your property to attract buyers in the current market. I'll talk more about the best presentation to maximise the sale price of your home later.

Method of sale

If the agent suggests a particular method of sale, ask them why it's best suited to your property. Unfortunately, most agents assume the vendors are reasonably *au fait* with the process of selling real estate. But most vendors aren't – they only do it a few times in their lives.

Get the agent to talk you through the process. Ask them, 'Let's assume I hand you a key when you walk out of here today, what happens next?' Ask them about a few properties they've sold recently. If they're suggesting an auction, ask them about a few properties they've taken to auction recently that haven't sold. 'Tell me a little bit about what happened with that property. Where do you think it came off the tracks?'

The agent should be able to tell you how long it's taking to sell a property on average in the current market ('days on market' as it's known in the trade). They will also be able to tell you their current auction clearance rate. You should also discuss how long it will take to prepare your marketing campaign and any repairs, maintenance and cleaning your property may need.

At this stage I wouldn't get too worried about trying to negotiate the agent's fee. I wouldn't even ask about commissions in the first round of interviews. Once you've chosen an agent who you feel is the best qualified, then you can talk to them about commission. The agent will also be able to give you costs of various marketing options.

Is there good chemistry?

As you're chatting to the agent, see if there's a good chemistry between you. Because the nature of the agent–vendor relationship is quite intimate and requires a lot of trust. You need a solid rapport, because you're going to be working very closely with your agent and you'll need a high degree of confidence in their recommendations and advice.

How is the agent's demeanour? Do they appear organised? Do they seem to have the tools of the trade? Did they call you in the morning to confirm the appointment? Did they arrive punctually? Did they have some research material ready? Did they have a coherent methodology for their sales presentation?

You definitely want to get some hard evidence on their track record. There's no doubt, an agent who has had a high degree of success selling properties similar to yours in your neighbourhood is a good contender. If your property is a little bit unique, however, that doesn't mean that a highly capable agent who doesn't have a lot of experience selling your particular style of property won't do a fabulous job.

Unusual properties

When I was selling, I used to love the opportunity to sell something a little out of the ordinary. One month I'd be selling a converted church, and the next I'd be selling a loft apartment. I've sold school halls and residences above shops. When I was asked to sell a property that was a little bit left-field, I had the basic sales capability and a huge enthusiasm, and I was prepared to do some research, all of which enabled me to do a good job for the vendors.

I wouldn't say that you should not consider an agent if they haven't had experience selling your style of property. However, a query about the agent's track record is a good way to get a feel for their experience and credentials.

Don't get too fixated on how long the agent has been in the business, because the industry has changed so much over the last 10 years. Having been in the industry for 20 years is no longer necessarily an advantage. Sometimes it can be a disadvantage. A lot of people who started at the same time I did have resisted the Internet, new technology and buyer databases, and are still doing ads the old-fashioned way.

Qualities of a good agent

You know you're dealing with a good agent when:

* they always have time for you and return your calls promptly

* they know your neighbourhood like the back of their hand

* they can supply you with a list of recent vendor references

* the agent is a model of honesty and integrity

* they're assertive enough to help you make decisions, but not so aggressive as to try to make decisions for you

* they are a skilful and confident negotiator.

Check their references

The number of clients the agent has sold for recently is a good reference point. I would be inclined to query them about their last few months' sales, and ask whether there's any chance they could give you the names of these vendors, and then, with their permission, you could call to have a chat with them.

This is really the acid test. A good agent will be delighted to give you a list of recent sellers. After all, it's an integral part of the agent's job to please their clients. If the agent starts making excuses, you can put a big question mark against their name. And if the agent is forthcoming with some names, a few quick phone conversations will give you the best feedback possible.

How's the marketing?

It's also a good idea to get an indication of the quality of the agent's marketing. Look at their ads in the newspaper. How is the look and feel? Do they have an attractive layout and appealing pictures? Does the copy read well?

Browse through the agent's website as though you were a buyer. What's the experience like? Is there a comprehensive list of properties, good data and tools that would help you if you were a buyer? Does it appear current, or are there listings in your neighbourhood that you know have sold three or four weeks ago?

These days, a specific discussion around Internet marketing strategy is important. You need an agent who is going to list your property on their website and the major real estate portals such as realestate.com.au and domain.com.au. But be aware, a website is not a solution to a problem, it's just one part of the marketing mix. And, to be effective, the website needs to be getting plenty of traffic. So I'd ask the question, 'What's the traffic to your website?'

Top 10 questions to ask agents

* How long have you been working in this area?

* What comparable homes have you sold in this area lately?

* What is the state of the market?

* How long is it taking you to sell well-priced listings at the moment?

* How much is my home worth? How have you come up with that figure?

* Should I sell by auction or private treaty? Why?

* What marketing strategy do you suggest? Why?

* What will you do to introduce buyers to my property?

* How does my house present? What should I do to maximise the sale price?

* Do you have a list of recent vendors I can speak to?

Check out the office

Real estate, almost more than any other industry, is highly personalised. The result achieved when you sell your property is largely due to the skill and effort of your agent, not necessarily the office or company they work for. The person that you're going to interact with 99 per cent of the time is the sales agent.

The ideal combination is a skilful and motivated agent backed by a customer-service orientated company that has integrity and a solid team of energetic people. A good real estate office has a high degree of teamwork. It's everything from following up buyers, organising the contract, putting the property on the Internet, setting up the marketing, organising the photographers, taking care of all the fine details, and briefing the other sales agents so they can introduce the property to their clients as well.

So when you're considering appointing an agent, I think it's a good idea to check out their office environment. I suggest visiting their office unannounced. Just drop by and see if they're in. How are you greeted at the reception area? What's the energy in the office like? Is the office neat and well organised? What's the calibre of the agent's colleagues?

How does the agent appear in their office? Because, just like a job interview, every agent will turn up for your interview with shiny shoes and a tie, and mentally well prepared. They've rehearsed their pitch and everything sounds good. But if you go to their office and the agent is in a flap, running late to appointments, and their office staff don't seem to have a lot of care for the people who arrive on their doorstep, you've got a mismatch.

AGENT'S FEES AND AGREEMENTS

The agreement that you sign with your chosen agent is known as an agency agreement. It lays out the rights and responsibilities of the vendor and agent, and gives the agent the authority to sell the property. There is a range of different real estate agency agreements. Each different type of agreement has different implications for your rights and responsibilities, how much commission you'll pay and to who, and how the property can be sold.

The type of agreement can also have significant ramifications for how efficiently your property is sold and how much money you receive for it. So it's important to choose wisely to save yourself a great deal of stress, and to make sure you maximise the sale price.

AGENCY AGREEMENTS

There are seven basic agency agreement types:

Exclusive agency agreement – you give one agent the right to sell your property by private treaty. Even if you or some other person sells the property, you must still pay the commission to the agent.

Auction agency agreement – as above, except the property is sold at auction.

Sole agency agreement – the same as an exclusive agency agreement, except the owner can sell their property privately without paying the agent's commission.

Open agency agreement – you employ a number of agents across the marketplace, but only the agent who sells your property receives the commission.

Multiple listing agency agreement – your chosen agent works with a cooperative network of agents to sell your home. Commonly known as 'multi-list', this type of agreement is rapidly becoming a dinosaur, as many of the participating agents are increasingly unwilling to list their best properties this way.

Co-agency – you hire two agents and they split the commission, regardless of which one makes the sale.

Conjunction agreement – one agent deals with the vendor and another agent deals with the buyer. These agreements usually occur when an agent wants to introduce a buyer to the listing agent.

Open agency

Open agency is a fairly dated approach to selling real estate. It came about in the days when there was good reason to believe that, in order to access all buyers, you needed to list your property with a number of agents to give yourself coverage. Nowadays, with cost-effective marketing tools such as the Internet, and with more vendors prepared to invest a little bit of money upfront for marketing the property, the need to share the listing with multiple agents is gone.

Open agency tends to reduce the incentives and accountability for agents – which is bad news for sellers. If you list your home with six agents, they all get excited for a week, bring every buyer they can find through your home and there's a mad race to get an offer. Then, all of a sudden, the next listing comes into their life and they get distracted by that.

Three weeks later, you haven't heard from any of them. You ring them up and there's no accountability, because they know you've got the property listed with five other agents and they're busy taking care of other clients. Step into the agent's shoes for a moment. Would you give priority to an open listing with a one-in-six chance of getting a commission, or would you give priority to an exclusive listing that you're guaranteed to get a commission for if the property sells?

Another potential problem with open agency is that it can become a race for the agents to sell the home first. Rather than finding you a buyer who will pay top dollar, the agent's challenge is to get a buyer – any buyer – over the line before any of the other agents do. Thus an agent may try to convince you to take any offer they may have (even if it's a low one) before another agent finds a buyer. Multiple agents' signboards in front of the property can also give buyers the impression your home is hard to sell – that is, there's something wrong with it.

Best practice

I don't know any agents who take on sole agency agreements, because there's a risk all their work will count for nothing if the vendor finds a buyer. If the agent puts a signboard out front and someone knocks on the door and negotiates a deal directly with the vendor, the agent has a problem, because they've just lost out on their fee.

These days, the most common forms of agreement are exclusive agency or auction agency agreements. In fact, you'll probably find most of the best agents will only agree to an exclusive agreement. By offering a single agent the entire commission to sell your property, you're giving them maximum incentive, because they know their effort will not be wasted.

Co-agency

I'm not a great fan of co-agency agreements because in most instances all they do is halve the incentive and, in my experience, one of the two agents ends up doing the majority of the work. However, there are some situations suited to co-agencies. If you have a reasonably unique property and you feel there are two likely target markets, and there are two different companies that have a good 'in' with those markets, you can benefit from a co-agency.

For example, if you were selling a beach house in Palm Beach (about one hour's drive north of Sydney's CBD), obviously you'd want to cover the local market, but you'd also probably want to cover the Sydney market too. So you could appoint an agent close to the CBD and an agent in Palm Beach, because they have the ability to introduce buyers from two different, but very relevant and important, markets.

Contract of sale

A residential property cannot be advertised for sale until a contract of sale has been drawn up. A draft contract must be available at the agent's office for buyers to inspect. Consult your solicitor or conveyancer to get everything in order.

THE FINE PRINT

The agency agreement is a legally binding contract, so it's important to give it a thorough once-over before you sign. The statutory requirements differ from state to state, so it's worth investigating what terms and conditions the agency agreement must include by law.

Typically, the agreement will cover the following issues:

✳ what services the agent will provide for you

✳ the amount of commission for the agent

✳ the circumstances in which the agent is entitled to payment of the commission – the commission is usually only payable when the property is sold

✳ how and when the agent's commission will be paid (e.g. can the agent deduct their commission from the buyer's deposit?)

✳ the extent of the agent's authority to act for you (e.g. can the agent make changes to the contract of sale or exchange contracts on your behalf?)

✳ the amount of money to be spent on marketing

✳ the duration of the agency agreement and how it can be ended early

✳ in some states, the agency agreement may need to include the agent's estimated selling price or price range and the amount of rebate and discounts they receive for any expenses they incur on your behalf (e.g. advertising space or cleaning, maintenance or landscaping services).

If you have any queries about the terms of the agreement, it's prudent to get legal advice.

You can negotiate the terms and length of the agency agreement, as well as the agent's commission. There is no minimum or maximum term for the agreement. It can even be open-ended (but then it must state how it can be ended).

Your decision on how long to commit to an agent should be based on your assessment of how long it will take them to get the job done. You don't have to give them a 12-month exclusive agreement. I recommend somewhere between one and three months – a reasonable time to get the price that you've agreed on.

Keep in mind that there is no automatic right to cancel the contract because you've changed your mind or are not happy with the job the agent is doing. Typically, you'll have to give 30 days' notice to end the agency agreement.

If things go sour

If an issue with the agent arises during the sale period, check your copy of the agency agreement to clarify your rights and obligations. It's best to try to sort out the problem by talking to the agent first. If that is unsuccessful, you could take your complaint to the principal of the company.

If you decide not to continue with the agent, be sure to terminate your relationship properly, according to the agency agreement (usually you must give notice). Don't take on another agent until the previous agency agreement is terminated or you could be liable to pay two commissions.

YOU GET WHAT YOU PAY FOR

Vendors often assume that if they negotiate a lower commission from an agent, then they're getting a better deal. In fact they may be getting a worse deal. They may pay a lower agent's fee, but a cut-price agent can end up getting them less money for their property than a more 'expensive' agent could have.

Just like all other goods and services, you get what you pay for. You're never going to walk into a clothing boutique and expect the best quality garments in the best fabrics to be anything but the most expensive. But you get to enjoy the benefits of that quality long after the purchase price has been paid.

It's the same with agent's fees. Most agents in Australia charge somewhere between 1 and 3 per cent commission. But the majority of highly capable agents are probably in the 2 to 3 per cent range. It may seem exorbitant for one agent to charge two or even three times more than another to sell your home. But when you consider that a good agent can add 10 to 15 per cent to the sale price in the negotiation phase alone, the extra commission is justified.

My advice is to not get too fixated on the agent's commission. Expect that you'll be offered a range of commissions, and that the best agents are probably going to be at the upper end of that range. Choose the best agent, not the lowest commission.

A good agent will more than earn the money they charge you by getting you a premium price for your property. I used to say to my clients, 'Look, if you think there's someone better than me to sell your property and they charge 1 per cent more than me, my recommendation would be to go with them. Because if they're that good, they'll be able to make you more than that 1 per cent extra in the first week of selling your property'.

Did the agent fold on their fee?

Like almost everything in real estate, agent's fees are negotiable. For example, say I was asking for 2.5 per cent, sometimes clients would say, 'Well, XYZ Real Estate was at 1.5 per cent'. And my response would be, 'I understand that, but how hard was it for you to negotiate their fee down to 1.5 per cent?' Because the way the agent negotiates their commission is a good indication of how they will negotiate with buyers for your home.

Did the agent just collapse at the first sign of resistance? Did they say, 'Well, I charge 2.5 per cent, but look, if you've had a quote for 1.5 per cent, I'll match it'? If they fold that easily when they're negotiating with their money, how will they go when it's your money at stake? What happens when your price is set at $400 000 and a buyer offers $360 000? Are they going to fold then too?

If an agent is really good, they may not negotiate their commission at all. If they're a skilful and confident agent, they may be able to ask for, and get, their price. However, they should be able to justify their premium commission with quantifiable evidence. Every agent will tell you they will work hard for you and get you the best price, but can they back up their claim?

A good agent won't try to coerce you into paying a higher commission. Good agents make their money by selling more homes for better prices, not by charging more or aggravating vendors.

Tiered selling commission

The commission is the agent's reward for doing their job successfully. But in some cases it may be appropriate to offer the agent an additional incentive for outstanding results. If the agent will go the extra distance to get you an exceptional price, it's not unreasonable to share a portion of the spoils with them.

A tiered commission offers such an incentive to agents. These commissions are calculated in two different ways. If you're expecting $400 000, you might pay a 2 per cent commission up to $410 000, and 3 per cent if the home sells above that. The agent gets a 50 per cent bonus if they can get a price that both of you agree is a good result. Alternatively, you might offer the agent 2 per cent up to $410 000 and 20 per cent of the balance above that.

If you're considering negotiating a tiered selling commission, make sure you have a good handle on values. If you set the base amount at an unachievable price, there's no incentive for the agent. And if you set it too low, you'll be paying extra commission unnecessarily.

MARKETING YOUR HOME

In the past there has been some scepticism about spending money on marketing a home for sale. People would say, 'The agents aren't going to trick me into spending money on marketing'. Vendors would often consider money spent on marketing an unnecessary cost.

Thankfully those attitudes have changed quite a bit. Nowadays vendors are a lot savvier about marketing and they can appreciate the benefits of it. Rather than an unwanted expense, they view marketing as contributing to the potential profit on the sale: If you're selling a home, you want it to be where the buyers are – that's what marketing is all about.

I think you should be open-minded about marketing your property. Ask yourself, 'If I was buying a property today, what would I do?' Most people would open up the local paper and then take a drive around the area they wanted to buy in and look for signboards. A lot of buyers now make the real estate Web portals their first port of call.

HOW MUCH AND HOW OFTEN?

In the old days, you'd only do marketing if you were selling by auction. If you sold by private treaty, you wouldn't. The reasoning was that for an auction to be successful, you needed to create maximum buyer interest in a brief period of time (usually 30 days) to stimulate competitive bidding on the day. There's no point having an auction if you're going to keep it a secret. You really want to go out there and market the property well.

Whereas with a private treaty the timeline is open-ended, so there's not the same urgency to find buyers. Because there's no deadline, agents could introduce buyers to the property as they made enquiries to the office. But, these days, more and more private treaty vendors are prepared to spend some money on marketing to quickly generate interest in the home.

There's nothing wrong with a degree of competitiveness around a private treaty listing. In fact, it's exactly what you want. I find that the minute I've got one buyer interested in a private treaty property, I'll always get one or two more. The energy of the sale just seems to change once one buyer is interested.

In my experience, the time a property gets the most attention is the first 14 to 21 days it's on the market. So if you're going to invest in marketing, I'd do most of it in the first 21 days to make a big initial impact and try and create some competitiveness amongst buyers, even if it isn't an auction sale.

Most vendors invest about 1 per cent of the value of their property in marketing, and I think that's a good rule of thumb. A 1 per cent marketing budget is effective across most price ranges. For anything from $250 000 to $2.5 million, the 1 per cent rule of thumb seems to be about right.

My recommendation is to start with a signboard and Internet listing, and then add other elements on top of that. Depending on what your budget allows, you can add local and metropolitan newspaper ads, agent's magazines and a brochure. The various options are as follows.

Signboards

My statistics show that around 60 per cent of buyers come from the local area – either the same suburb, an adjoining suburb or within 5 to 10 kilometres. And buyers from outside the area almost always come into the area before buying. They're visiting open homes, driving around to check out the housing stock and the best locations, and walking the streets to soak up the vibe.

Buyers are consciously on the lookout for signboards, so they're an excellent way to attract attention. They are a very cost-effective marketing tool. For $200 to $300, you can generate a huge amount of enquiries.

Those people who enquire about a home after seeing a signboard are generally very qualified buyers. They've already bought the location – if they didn't like the location they wouldn't have rung in the first place. They're probably pretty keen on the style of the property as well.

Vendors who put a premium on their privacy are sometimes hesitant about signboards. They don't necessarily want all their neighbours knowing they're selling. They might feel a bit uncomfortable about everyone knowing their reason for selling, such as a divorce or financial issue.

What I typically would say to those people is that I have no issue with selling property without a signboard. But the reality is that people will find out you're selling anyway. The minute an agent arrives with a buyer and takes them through the home, people will start talking. Neighbours work out pretty quickly that your property is on the market. But without a signboard you're missing out on attracting a lot of qualified buyers.

Selling on the quiet

There's no right or wrong way to market your home. It all depends on the property and your circumstances. When I sold my last inner-city apartment, I wanted the sale process to be fairly discreet. At that stage of my life I preferred not to open my home for inspection and I preferred not to have the sale splashed across the newspapers.

I chose to restrict the marketing to the Internet because I felt the apartment would suit an expat buyer. I invested about $500 for photography and the Internet listing. I ended up selling it to a local buyer for a price I was ecstatic with.

Internet

The Internet has totally revolutionised the way people buy property. It offers unparalleled convenience and coverage of the market. It makes home hunting vastly more efficient and gives vendors an expanded range of options to market their properties.

Real estate websites are often the first place buyers look for a new home. They're attracted to the convenience and the ease of browsing up-to-the-minute listings in the comfort of their own homes at a time that suits them. Many people sign up for automatic e-mail alerts that inform them when a new property fitting their criteria hits the market.

For $200 or $300 you can get your property listed on the best real estate portals in Australia and market to buyers from around the country and abroad. It's a very cost-effective method of accessing buyers who are looking for properties in your suburb.

Virtual tours are a terrific online selling tool. They give serious buyers an excellent look at the property. We sell four or five properties a month to overseas buyers who never inspect the home in person. They view the floor plan and take a virtual tour on the Web. They might know the location and they can e-mail or speak to the agent to check the details. They can gather enough information online and over the phone to form a sufficiently confident opinion of the property to put in an offer.

My recommendation is that Web listings are complementary to traditional display advertising, rather than an alternative. Traditional local media is still extremely effective, but its impact can be boosted by Web marketing.

Newspapers

If your budget allows, I would definitely run a display ad in the local paper. The value of advertising in the local paper is really the visual element. A picture, as they say, is worth a thousand words. Some flattering pictures of your property will go a long way towards stimulating buyer interest and will help set it apart from other properties advertised.

Obviously the advantage of metropolitan dailies such as *The Sydney Morning Herald, The Age, The West Australian* or the *Courier-Mail* is that they have a wider reach. Since 60 per cent of the buyers come from the local area, a local paper and signboard strategy is a very good one. But with around 40 per cent of your buyers coming from some other part of town, another state or country, you want to make sure that you've got their attention as well.

The metropolitan papers are predominantly a classified directory, so you don't necessarily need to go for a display ad, although many people do use them very effectively.

Brochures

I think every good property deserves a good brochure. I'm a big fan of floor plans, because they give buyers something to stay excited about once they've left the inspection. They have something they can share with their partner if they didn't see the home.

I've seen many people arrive for a second inspection with their sketches and notes all over the floor plan. They've actually remodelled the entire home. They've drawn all their furniture in and they've thought to themselves, 'This can be Johnny's room and this is Mary's room and we could put a deck here ...' Which means that from the time I first showed them the home, they haven't stopped thinking about it.

Keeping buyers excited about the property is very good for the sale. It helps to maintain the momentum, and buyers begin to take ownership of the home in their minds. So floor plans are a valuable marketing tool. Typically they cost between $100 and $200 for an average house, and I think that's a very worthwhile investment.

Flyers and letterbox drops

Producing a flyer and arranging a letterbox drop throughout your suburb is a good strategy for flushing out any buyers from the neighbourhood. The flyers complement the signboard, but their reach can also extend beyond the suburb's boundaries.

Often people in your area have friends, relatives or work colleagues who are interested in moving into the neighbourhood. So a flyer is something tangible your neighbours can give to their friends who are looking to buy in the area. They can take it to work, mail it to their friend or ring them up and discuss it over the phone.

Real estate magazines

Our company did the first real estate magazine in Sydney. The idea came to me one day when I was showing a home in Paddington. I was talking to a buyer and he said, 'This one's not for me, John – what else have you got?'

I had a few other properties listed that I thought he might be interested in, so I pulled a card out of my pocket and I wrote a few addresses on the back of it. I handed to him and I said, 'Why don't you go and have a look at these ones?' But at the time I was thinking, 'That's not the most professional way to do this'. I had terrible handwriting, for a start!

That was in the first few years of my selling career, and in those days our marketing wasn't terribly sophisticated. We'd type up a brochure on our letterhead and glue our own photograph of the property on it. Then we'd put that on the photocopier and run off a few dozen copies. It was all very crude.

I decided that next time around I'd get the brochures for all of our listings and I'd staple them together. So if a buyer came through and didn't like the home I was representing, I'd hand them a selection of other properties. It seemed to make sense, it was customer-friendly and, at the time, quite unique.

I started doing that and it became so popular people would look for me at open homes and ask, 'Can I get all your brochures?' Then I went to an instant printing company and got a quote for printing up all the brochures, putting them in a cover and rolling out a couple of hundred copies every week.

And that was how *Space* magazine was born. Nowadays it's much more sophisticated, with a magazine-style layout in glossy colour, perfect bound on high-quality paper stock. Because it's an attractive magazine, people will pick up a copy, take it home or to a café, and have a good browse through it.

It's proven to be a very effective marketing vehicle. One of our agents at our Sydney Northern Beaches office told me that over 50 per cent of his buyers in 2003 came from *Space* magazine. Buyers are looking to buy a lifestyle and are now far more flexible about where they'll buy than they ever have been in the past. A well-produced magazine enables you to present the lifestyle aspect of your property in an appealing way to a wide selection of buyers.

QUALITY COUNTS

So far I've been telling you about what marketing materials you can use to attract buyers' attention. Now I want to discuss the quality of the marketing materials – the layout, photography and copywriting. Because your marketing not only alerts buyers that your property is for sale, it should also motivate them to take some action.

The purpose of the marketing is not to sell the property. The purpose of the marketing is to generate an interested enquiry and, ultimately, an inspection. It must present your property in an enticing way in order to stimulate a buyer's interest enough to phone your agent or attend an inspection. Your ad, signboard and brochure don't do the selling – their job is to generate enquiries from interested buyers.

Your marketing gives buyers a feeling for the lifestyle potential of your property. Better quality marketing creates a more favourable impression. A lot of people often say to me (which I take as a great compliment), 'You guys only handle really nice properties'. In reality, we handle the same mix of properties as most of our competitors. But we make a great effort to present our properties better.

That comes down to expert styling and providing the vendor with contacts for good landscapers, cleaners, painters, etc. We make the job of preparing the home for the photographer (and buyers) incredibly easy for the vendor. We use top-notch photographers and they only shoot when the light is good. If the day is overcast, they'll reschedule. We have five professional copywriters who work on our properties full-time.

Less is more

A common mistake vendors make is insisting that every single feature of their home is mentioned in the marketing copy. Rather than listing every single feature, the copy should focus on the most attractive features that will have an emotional appeal for buyers. You might not mention the internal laundry or security alarm, but you'd want to emphasise the fireplaces, views, beautifully landscaped garden and pool.

A professional approach

The quality of marketing should be one of the deciding factors for choosing an agent. You don't have to be an expert to tell good marketing from bad. Simply go through the local paper and real estate websites and just ask yourself which ads stand out for you. I think you have to select an agent who takes a professional approach.

What typically captures a buyer's attention is the image and the address of the property. They clearly want to know the basic features – how many bedrooms, how many bathrooms, is there parking, is there a garden and so on. The style of the property typically comes through in the image of the home. Many agents use icons in their ads to denote how many bedrooms and bathrooms the property has (this information should be easy to see).

Most real estate copywriting is overflowing with clichés. It's best to have simple but emotive language that describes the essence of the property. I would tend towards less copy rather than more. Some agents write good copy, but it's usually best to use the services of a professional real estate copywriter. They're experts at inspiring buyers' interest with their words.

Collaborative effort

Insist on seeing all your marketing material before it goes to press. You should have the opportunity to assess the proposed marketing and give your feedback. It's important that you're happy with all the copy, photos and layout. Because if you're not comfortable, then all of a sudden you're going to get some tension in your relationship with the agent.

So read the copy, look at the images and the layout, and see how it feels for you. Is this how you want your property portrayed? Is the copy clear, concise and cliché-free? Does it make you want to find out more about the home? Do the photos show off your home's best features? Talk about any concerns with your agent and get them to make the necessary adjustments.

BUYER DATABASE

Most real estate agents receive dozens of buyers' enquiries every day. Buyers phone agents to follow up on an ad or a signboard they've seen, they'll register their interest about a particular listing on a website, or they'll walk in the front door and ask to speak to the agent directly.

These enquiries are a goldmine for agents, because if a buyer goes to the trouble of enquiring directly about a property, they are clearly qualified and motivated. The agent has the opportunity to quiz them about their wants and needs and introduce them to suitable properties they have on their books.

Good agents keep detailed records of all enquiries on a buyer database. Matching buyers on their database to the properties they have listed is the most targeted and effective form of marketing. So it's wise to choose an agent who keeps a current buyer database and uses it to introduce buyers to your property.

Do it yourself?

Around 2 per cent of vendors in Australia decide to sell their home themselves. If you're tempted to go it alone and save the agent's commission, you need to consider the challenges of FSBOs (for sale by owner):

* Can you make an objective assessment of the asking price for your property, based on recent comparable sales?

* Are you competent to produce compelling marketing material?

* Do you have the time to prepare and execute a marketing campaign and liaise with multiple buyers?

* Are you an experienced and skilful negotiator?

* Can you compare and contrast the features of your property with other properties that are currently for sale or have sold recently?

* Can you stay upbeat and motivated after dozens of buyers have turned down your own home that you love?

If you answered a confident 'yes' to all these questions, you're probably a good candidate for FSBO. But there are still compelling reasons to go with an agent. A good agent offers many resources that aren't available to owners, such as buyers' databases, property magazines, listings on real estate portals, and access to experienced copywriters and photographers.

Also, the opportunity cost of doing it yourself may be far greater than the amount you'd save, especially if you're a busy professional. I'm not against FSBOs, and I think some vendors could probably sell better than bad agents and save themselves some money in the process. But, for their experience, negotiation skills and marketing resources, I truly believe a good agent is outstanding value at 2 to 3 per cent commission.

STYLING FOR SALES SUCCESS

Presenting homes for sale has become something of an art of late, which is an excellent thing. With the proliferation of real estate reality shows on TV, people are seeing real-life examples of how a light makeover can dramatically boost the selling price. Styling has become quite a big business, with a large number of stylists who make their living from helping vendors present their property in its best light, to achieve a premium price.

Presentation is a critical part of the selling process. I use the metaphor of selling your car. You might wash your car every week, but if you're going to sell it this weekend, you'll probably put in a little more effort. You want to get it that little bit tidier, just that touch shinier. So you get the cotton buds out and clean all the nooks and crannies, and you take the Armour All out to get the tyres and trim looking like new.

It's the same when you sell your home. You want to make it as attractive as possible to buyers. In order to get top dollar for your property, it needs to be in tiptop shape. You don't need to hire a stylist – most of the things that improve a home's presentation you can do yourself. But hiring a professional is an interesting option if you have the budget.

Investing a little bit of time and money upfront to get the presentation of your home just right results in anything from a $5000 to a $50 000 upside in most instances that I've seen. So it's definitely worth your while.

Top five pre-sale presentation tactics

1. Tidy up the garden – a well-presented garden makes a big impression. A $500 garden makeover can definitely add $5000 to $10 000 if it's done right.

2. Detail the home – just as you would detail your car if you were going to sell it, you need to polish up your home. Get the windows sparkling, the carpet deodorised, water blast the grime off the exterior, etc.

3. Touch up the paintwork – paint is a reliable way to improve presentation. Don't use it to cover up sins, but a cosmetic coat of fresh paint is inexpensive and effective.

4. Styling – you don't need a professional, just get an objective opinion of what furniture and accessorising work, and what bits and pieces you'd be better without.

5. De-cluttering – a big part of styling is de-cluttering, so get rid of all your excess stuff. If your home appears clean, uncluttered and well organised, it takes away a lot of people's fears about problems lurking beneath the surface.

GET A SECOND OPINION

The first step in presenting a home for sale is to go over it from top to bottom and see what can be improved. What needs to be tidied up, what needs to be repaired, what needs to be cleaned, what needs to be thrown out and what needs to be replaced? Start a list and keep adding items as you notice them.

At this point it's also very helpful to get a friend, relative or an agent to look over the property with fresh eyes. You need an objective opinion, because you're probably a bit biased about your home's appearance. We all tend to exaggerate the good and ignore the bad. There are probably quite a few areas that need attention, but you're so used to them they slip under the radar.

An agent's opinion is invaluable because they'll be able to compare the presentation of your property with others in the market. They'll also know what gripes and objections buyers commonly have. Something that you may not even notice or think is a minor issue – chipped paint, a broken kitchen door handle, a few spots on the carpet – could be a sticking point for buyers.

Listen carefully to what you're told, as people are sometimes too polite to come straight out and give you barefaced feedback for fear of offending you. For example, the agent might say, 'Your home looks great, but it would really shine with a fresh coat of paint', or 'Some new kitchen cupboard doors would look great'. Keep an open mind, don't take any of the feedback too personally and listen carefully for any dropped hints.

The professionals

Hiring a stylist to spruce up your home for sale is now quite common – and not just for multimillion-dollar homes. A stylist can offer an objective view on how to present your home in its best light. A well-styled home increases the desire amongst buyers and can lead to a higher price. Costs for styling range from around $2000 to $10 000, and a stylist will usually give you a consultation and appraisal for a small fee.

Street appeal

Body-language experts tell us that when someone is sizing up another person as a potential love mate or employee they make a 'go/no-go' decision within the first few seconds of laying eyes on them. It's really not that much different with real estate. The impression your home makes on buyers when they first see it from the street is vitally important.

If their first impression is bad, buyers will often look for reasons to back up that impression as they inspect the home. Conversely, if their first impression is good they are more likely to look for reasons why they should buy the property. Also, buyers often do drive-by inspections. If a home doesn't capture their imagination immediately from the street, they may simply cross it off their list and move onto the next one.

A great way to assess your property's street appeal is to drive up to the home with some friends in the car and ask them what they first notice about the property and what they like don't like. Faded or peeling paintwork, dirty windows, a grimy exterior, falling-down fences and overgrown gardens are common turn-offs. Also, look at stains on the driveway, the condition of the front door, and squeaky or difficult-to-open front gates.

So, your first job is to attend to the property's street appeal. You may need to hire a water blaster to clean the front of the house, you may have to touch up some paint, or you may have to do a little bit of planting and hedge trimming. You want to make sure that when the signboard goes up and everyone starts looking at your home, they have a good feeling, and they want to take the next step and ring the agent or come for an inspection.

De-clutter

Clutter is the mortal enemy of good presentation. What you may see as cosy, many buyers will see as cluttered. Less clutter gives the impression of more space. It gives buyers room to imagine themselves and their belongings in the home, while still maintaining a livable feeling.

A typical mistake a lot of vendors make is over-furnishing. If you've been somewhere for 10 years, you probably started with a certain set of furniture and have collected more over the years. Often the home becomes a little bit overcrowded. Only a fresh set of eyes will see that, because you get so used to it.

Sometimes less is less

In some instances the problem isn't over-furnishing but under-furnishing. The first properties to sell in a new development are always the display apartments. It's not necessarily because they are better (in fact, they're often not the best apartments), but they look like a home rather than an empty space. People fall in love with the overall impression of a great lifestyle.

That's where stylists are useful. They can often organise to rent you suitable furniture for the sale period if your property is under-furnished. It can be quite a cost-effective way to lift the overall impression of the home.

Most people are going to sell or throw out their excess belongings when they move home. My recommendation is to make that decision 60 days before moving, that is, when you make up your mind to sell. If you're going to sell some furniture, take a load of junk to the tip, or have a garage sale, do it now rather than waiting till you actually move out.

If you don't want to part with your furniture, it's pretty simple to call up a removalist company and get them to store your furniture for a month or two. If you have a garage, give it a spring clean and clear out any excess junk. While you're at it, clear out the back yard. You can hire a trailer to take a few loads to the tip, or get a mini-skip.

Garden grooming

The garden is an incredibly important selling feature of a house. Many times when I've been showing a family home, I have seen that when the buyer stepped into the back yard the sale was made. They look around the garden and they visualise themselves there, having barbecues and playing with the kids. So you definitely need to make the outdoor area as attractive as possible.

Mow the lawn, trim the hedges and rake up all the leaves. Water restrictions permitting, put the sprinkler on the lawn to create a fresh and green appearance. Are your garden beds looking a bit tired? A few new shrubs can add a bit of colour to outdoor areas. Stow away kids' toys and garden tools, and de-clutter the garden shed.

If you have a deck, pergola or patio, make sure it's free of clutter too. Some tasteful outdoor furniture greatly adds to the appeal of outdoor living areas. If you have a pool, give it a good clean, but make sure you do it a few days before the first inspection because you don't want chlorine fumes to overpower the buyers.

Spic 'n' span

It goes without saying that your home should be spotlessly clean for the inspections, especially the bathroom and kitchen. Nothing turns a buyer off faster than kitchen walls and ceilings coated with grease or bathroom tiles caked with mould and soap scum. Now is the time to give your home a thorough spring clean. Could the carpet use a steam clean? Perhaps you need to get the sugar soap out and wash the handprints off the kids' bedroom walls.

Sparkling clean windows are essential. Dirty windows are equated with a dirty home in many buyers' minds. Clean windows will also maximise the natural light entering the home. If you can't do them all yourself, hire someone who can.

Light fittings accumulate lots of dust and dead bugs over time. Giving them a good clean will make your home much brighter and cheerier. You might also consider replacing any dated light fittings with more modern ones, which is a cost-effective way to give your home a fresh, modern touch.

Not everybody loves pets the way that you might, and pet smells are a major turn-off. Often you're so used to it you don't notice the smell any more. But buyers will. If your home has dog or cat odour, steam cleaning and deodorising the carpet and furniture is a must. Some vendors choose to board their pets at a kennel during the inspection period. For a lot of people pets are like their family, so it's a hard decision to make, but it's something you should consider.

If there's any minor repair work that needs to be done to the property – squeaking doors, dripping taps, cracked windowpanes, broken kitchen cupboard doors, etc. – it's worthwhile getting a handyman through to tidy all these things up (that's if you can't do them yourself). You can also get them to do any minor cosmetic changes that will add appeal. For example, some new vinyl or linoleum on the kitchen floor or some new shelves might really make the house shine.

I recommend people clear out all the junk and excess clothes from their built-in wardrobes. Because, like it or not, buyers will often open up wardrobes to have a look to see how much space there is. If your built-ins look neat and well organised, that leaves a positive impression.

PRE-SALE RENOVATION

Great presentation is all about creating an attractive appearance and an appealing atmosphere. You don't need to spend thousands of dollars to prepare your home for sale. In fact, it might be a financial mistake to do so.

Minor investments such as a new coat of paint, getting a handyman to attend to all the minor repairs and maintenance, or having the exterior cleaned with high-pressure water blasters can generate a great return in terms of a better price. The goal is to get the maximum price for your home while spending the least amount of money.

If your paintwork is looking a little dull, but your home is otherwise in good shape, I would consider a fresh coat of paint. If natural wear and tear is starting to show up – fingermarks, chipped architraves and trim, a few stains on the walls – you should consider tidying all that up. I don't recommend fresh paint to cover up sins, but it's a nice final touch before you get your buyers through.

When you're considering spending money to improve the presentation of your home for sale, it should come down to a simple cost/benefit analysis. How much will it cost to do the work and how much will it add to the price of your home? You also have to assess the time factor. It will take you some time to get the work done, but a freshly renovated home may sell more quickly. Also, do you have the time and energy to project manage the renovations?

Beware of overcapitalising

If you're planning substantial renovations, you have to be wary of overcapitalising. If the purpose of the renovations is to improve your enjoyment of your home, then by all means go for it. But if it's a pre-sale renovation, be aware that you won't necessarily recoup your investment at sale time. Not all home improvements add the same amount of value as they cost, and some can even diminish the value of the home.

Add value for less

Skylights are a great way to boost the value of your home without spending a lot of money. They're easy and quick to install, and add light and warmth. Most of the time you don't need council approval (but check first). Updating your floor coverings is another excellent value-add you can do without huge expense – anything from steam cleaning or replacing the carpet to pulling it up and polishing the floorboards.

Be careful with putting in a pool. It's a very expensive addition, around $50 000 nowadays, so you need to get a significant price hike to get your money back. Trouble is, a lot of buyers don't want pools. Pools require costly and time-consuming maintenance, and there are child safety issues. That doesn't appeal to a lot of people, especially in coastal belts where people often prefer to go to the beach if they want to swim.

Second-storey additions are a risky proposition for similar reasons. If it's going to suit you and your family and you'll get five years of use before you sell, it's an excellent thing to do. But some people think, 'We have a great location and a good house, but I reckon some buyers will find it a bit small. Let's go up and add another two bedrooms'. Well, guess what? The chances that you're going to pick the right style, finishes and configuration for the best next buyer are not high.

A better plan is to get an architect to draw plans for the extension. You can even get a development application approved from council. That way, for a small outlay, you've shown the potential of the property and given buyers the option to expand if they wish.

FIXER-UPPERS

If your property is old, unrestored and in need of a complete makeover, it's not necessary to change that. I think there's actually a huge amount of appeal in a 'fixer-upper' or 'renovator's delight'. I've often found that fixer-uppers fetch almost the same prices as similar properties that have been renovated.

People are often very keen to get into a sought-after neighbourhood and/or they want a property they can renovate exactly to their own tastes. In these situations there's often not a huge differential in price between renovated and unrenovated homes that are otherwise alike.

At an auction, you'll typically find more competition for an unrenovated than a renovated home for two reasons. Firstly, most buyers underestimate the cost of renovation. They think they can do it for $10 000 and it ends up costing them $20 000. If they'd known that when they started bidding, they probably wouldn't have paid what they did.

Secondly, it's like the movie *Ghost* – when the young lovers saw that big old warehouse apartment they got totally immersed in the fantasy of renovating it. They could seem themselves painting, and dust flying off the walls as they transformed it into their ideal nest. People love the idea of getting exactly what they want rather than accepting what the last owner wanted.

Fixer-upper options

If you want to sell a fixer-upper, there are three choices open to you:

1. leave it as is and sell as a renovator's delight

2. give it a light makeover for cosmetic effect

3. fix it up completely – but make sure you do your cost/benefit analysis first.

OPEN HOMES OR BY APPOINTMENT?

You'll have to decide whether you would like to open your home to the general public for inspection or let your agent arrange buyers to inspect the home by appointment. I don't necessarily think one way is better than the other, but when I'm buying I really love open homes.

A lot of properties I've bought have been from a spur-of-the-moment decision to go to an open home. I've been browsing the property section of Saturday's paper over breakfast when a property has caught my eye. I've thought to myself, 'Wow, that looks great. I'm going to check that out at midday.'

Open-home inspections are convenient and allow buyers to be spontaneous. If I'd had to ring up an agent and make a specific appointment to go and see it, my excitement would have waned and I would probably never have bothered to inspect the property.

Because there are several (maybe dozens) of buyers congregated at an open home, it can create a bit of excitement amongst the buyers – it gets their competitive juices flowing, and that's good for the selling price. It's also easier to clean up the home for twice-weekly opens than keeping it clean all the time in case the agent calls and wants to bring a buyer around.

However, inspection by appointment does have its place. If your property isn't highly attractive from outside, but a gem on the inside, inspections by appointment may be the better option. It's less likely buyers will drive by and reject the home from the street without inspecting it, and during the inspection the agent will be able to emphasise the best features of the home. Inspection by appointment can also be good for small homes, because too many people at one time can make the home seem smaller.

Inspection time

On inspection day do all the washing-up, make all the beds and tidy up all mess. Turn on all the lights and open all the curtains and blinds. Giving buyers a positive impression is all about creating an inviting ambience. So for me, presentation goes right down to the music that you play at the inspections. I would always choose some music to play based on the sort of buyers I expect to arrive at the open home.

Some people go to the extent of placing fresh flowers throughout the home, brewing a pot of coffee, or baking or buying fresh bread. It goes towards creating an ambience and suggesting a certain lifestyle, and I think there's a place for it all. You have to treat buyers with respect. You don't want to try to hoodwink them or trick them, because buyers are more sophisticated than they've ever been. But there's nothing wrong with adding a little bit of theatre to the process to enhance their experience.

A lot of people say winter is a bad time to sell. But for some properties it's a great time to sell. I've sold terrace houses a lot of my life and I've found that many of them look their best when they've got a crackling fire going. It creates a cosy atmosphere on a wintry day. The garden is not the major element of a terrace house – it's more about the interior and the cosiness.

While it's tempting to hang around and have a stickybeak at the people who might be moving into your home, it's best to leave your home while the inspections are on. Buyers generally feel more comfortable when the owners aren't around. They can talk freely amongst themselves. A good agent will always give you an update on buyer feedback after each inspection.

Security first

Don't forget, dozens of strangers will be roaming through your property on each inspection day and there is a risk of theft on the day or sometime later. While your agent and their helper will be conscious of the security of your property and possessions, they don't have eyes in the backs or their heads.

It's sensible to take few simple precautions. Lock away or remove all your valuables, especially small items such as jewellery, wallets and camera equipment. It's also prudent to check if your insurance policy covers you for home inspections.

THE PRICE IS RIGHT

Pricing is probably the most difficult part of the selling process for vendors to come to grips with. A vendor's biggest challenge is usually understanding and getting comfortable with the fair market value of their home.

HOW THE SELLING PRICE IS DETERMINED

The cardinal rule of pricing is that the selling price for your home is determined by the buyers. You put an asking price on it, but the selling price is what a buyer is willing and able to pay. It's not unlike the stock market. If you're selling shares, you can ask whatever price you want. But until you actually meet the buyers' bids, there's not going to be a transaction. You can say, 'Well, I want $10 for my BHP shares'. But if the buyers are at $9.50, guess what? You have to meet the buyers or you won't sell.

Now you can sell a property for any price ... eventually. Over time, the effect of inflation will bring buyers' offers towards a vendor's overly optimistic asking price. But whether that's in two months or two years is the crucial question. How long are you prepared to wait to get your price?

After getting the highest price for their home, a vendor's next biggest concern is selling within a reasonable time frame. Few vendors want to have their home languishing on the market for months on end. Pricing is the key to a quick sale. Like it or not, the property market is very price sensitive. Buyers want to get the most bang for their buck. If you price the home right, buyers will come.

Your home can have many appealing features. But nothing will be more attractive to a buyer than an attractive price. If you put your home on the market for more than buyers perceive it's worth, it can languish without offers, even in a booming market. Similarly, you can sell quickly, even in a stagnant market, if you price the home slightly below the value buyers perceive it at.

What does *not* determine the price of your home:

✳ how much you hope you can get

✳ how much the neighbours think you'll get

✳ how much you need to get to pay off your mortgage, divorce settlement, new home, etc.

✳ how much money you spent renovating your home

✳ how much you love your home.

PERCEIVED VALUE

If you got six property valuers to value your home tomorrow, they would most likely come back with a fairly tight range of valuations, say, for example, from $680 000 to $720 000. Valuers use a formula based on factors such as comparable historical sales, the size of the land and home, the condition of the home and improvements, and so on. Obviously there is some room for individual interpretation, hence the range of valuations.

Now, if I got six buyers to look at your home, they might price it from $650 000 to $750 000. Buyers work out their offers based on the selection of homes they have seen and what they know about the current market. It comes down to perceived value. Buyers will have a range of prices they are willing to pay for your home, based on their own assessments of the market, your property and its presentation, market demand and how much they like it and want to own it.

The trouble is, until you start receiving offers, you can never be sure what a buyer is willing to pay. All you can do is to find out what other buyers have recently paid for similar homes. Setting an asking price comes down to making comparisons – it's more of an art than a science. No two homes are identical, so you must compare your home to similar homes and adjust for any differences. How does your home stack up against other similar homes in the neighbourhood that have sold recently?

Vendor's self appraisal

While buyers have their perceived value for a home, vendors also perceive their home to have a certain value. But very often a vendor's self appraisal will be totally out of line with the market. It's natural to be proud of your home and to want to get a high price for it, but that can make you biased. A little pride mixed with a dash of misinformation can put your expectations way above fair market value.

Most people have in mind a figure for what their home is worth. They know how much they paid for it and how much they've spent renovating. They may have some idea of how much the property market has been going up lately, and a few of the prices paid for some other homes in the neighbourhood recently. But all of this is no substitute for comparable market evidence.

There's also the emotional investment vendors have in their home. They have a history with the place, so it's much harder for them to be objective. They've put their love, effort and money into creating their own little haven. They've grown up there or watched their family grow up there, and had a wealth of experience in the home. A buyer simply doesn't have that emotional connection. They can like the home, but they see it a little bit more objectively than a seller who has lived there for the last 10 years.

Vendors also often have a strong sense of attachment to their homes because they've decorated them to suit their tastes. Everything is exactly where they want it and looking as they like it. However, that particular configuration and décor probably won't suit the entire market. What you may perceive as highly desirable and valuable, a potential buyer may view as a drawback (and a possible source of expense to rectify).

What the neighbours say

Many people who are thinking of selling their home confer with their neighbours. The neighbour says, 'You'd have to get a million plus for a home like yours today'. Which is music to your ears, since you were thinking $850 000 to $900 000. 'That dump down the road went for $750 000,' they say. In fact, it was listed for $750 000 but actually sold for $690 000.

Of course the neighbour has a vested interest in talking up the prices in the neighbourhood. Everyone likes to think they're sitting on prime real estate. When your neighbour tells you you'll get a high price, their valuation will often reflect the value they put on their own home (which is also probably a bit exaggerated), rather than any actual current market evidence. So you can't really trust what the neighbours think.

In order to set a realistic asking price, you must be prepared to put aside all your preconceptions and everything you've heard. Keep an open mind and objectively analyse the current sales data. The fair market value of your home might be less than what you want for it or think it's worth. But it's better to find that out now, rather than when you've spent thousands on marketing, had weeks of inspections and received no offers. Have a look at the facts and see if you can live with the price you're likely to get.

Chinese whispers

About 15 years ago I sold an ultra-modern house in Sydney's blue-ribbon waterfront suburb of Point Piper. The owners called the office to see if we might have an interested buyer. We actually did have an interested buyer who lived in the same neighbourhood. They made an offer around $11 million, but negotiations stalled, so we went to market.

We did an $80 000 marketing campaign, which generated some enquiries and some inspections. Six weeks later we sold it to the neighbour for $11.25 million. Some people thought the owners had wasted their money doing marketing. But in fact the marketing helped to confirm the price was right (because we couldn't get a better offer), and put pressure on the buyer to pay a little bit more (which covered the marketing expenses).

The interesting thing was that when I first met the owner he said he'd had interest of $15 million from Elton John, but he pulled out. Obviously that was informing his expectations. Subsequently I found out that Elton John had been on a harbour cruise, seen the house and said, 'That's a beautiful home – what would that be worth?' Someone, perhaps the cruise director or another passenger, said that it would probably be worth about $15 million.

Apparently Elton said something like, 'Gee, I'd like to buy a home like that in Sydney'. Now that ended up, through Chinese whispers, translating to Elton John offering $15 million. I guess what comes out of this story is you have to be a little bit careful about misinformation and third-hand innuendo about property values.

AGENT'S VALUATION

To work out a realistic asking price for your home, you'll need to do a little research. One of the best places to start is to ask the agents you interviewed for their assessment of its value. But, when you get the agent's valuations, remember that agents aren't professional valuers. Their valuation will be based on their working knowledge of the local property market and recent sales data. Furthermore, it may be in their interest to give you a high valuation if it means they'll get your business. So it's best to take the agent's valuation with a pinch of salt – trust, but verify.

The agent should be able to back up their valuation with some current market evidence. Just because an agent's given you a list of recent sales doesn't mean they're comparable to your home. Ask the agent to go over their analysis of your home's value. You can start up the conversation with, 'Tell me about some of the properties that have sold recently, and how they compare with my home'. You want them to talk you through why they believe the homes are comparable.

When I was selling, sometimes I used to physically take some of my potential vendors through recent homes I'd sold. I'd ring up the owners and say, 'Is there any chance I could bring a couple through your home, because they've got a really similar property they're thinking of selling, and I reckon they'll get a similar price. Would you mind?' A lot of my vendors had no problem with that.

Open homes

Open-home inspections aren't just for buyers. They provide a wealth of information for sellers too. It can be a valuable experience for vendors to think like a buyer and spend a couple of Saturdays seeing what's on the market and what prices are being achieved. The key issue to consider is, 'How does this property compare with mine?' By following up sale prices of comparable homes, you can quickly establish a realistic price range for your own home.

The key word is 'comparable'. If it's not recent, it's not comparable – the market may have shifted significantly. If it hasn't sold, it's not comparable – because the asking price is not the selling price. If it's not similar, it's not comparable – similar means similar land size, style, condition, location, views and aspect. It doesn't have to be identical, because you can adjust for small differences, but it needs to be similar.

If you get out in the market and acquire some first-hand knowledge of prices, you'll be able to verify the agent's valuation. When an agent says, 'This one down the road went for $700 000', you can say, 'Yeah, but that one didn't have a garage and didn't have a view and it only had one bathroom'. If you've seen 10 to 20 comparable properties, then you're really going to know values.

Time savers

The difference between buyers and vendors is that buyers usually spend a longer time getting acquainted with the market. A buyer will often take four to six weeks to find a property. Vendors, however, often make up their minds to sell and a week later they're talking to agents. They don't have much time to get a handle on values.

So my advice is the moment you start thinking about selling, start doing some research on prices. Look up the sales results in the property pages of the weekend newspapers. Log onto a real estate portal and search for similar properties for sale in your neighbourhood and sign up for e-mail alerts. Agents' websites often have details of recent sales.

Get a 12-month sales report for your suburb from Australian Property Monitors or Residex. Chances are you'll be familiar with some of the homes that have sold recently. With your report in hand, you can do a drive-by inspection of all the homes that have sold in the neighbourhood and you'll start to get a good idea of fair market value.

Independent valuation

If you want to double-check your research, or if you don't have the time to inspect comparable homes, a great strategy is to get an independent valuer to appraise your home. Valuers are highly trained and totally unbiased, since they have no vested interest in the sale of your home. For an investment of a few hundred dollars, you'll get a written appraisal which gives you the confidence to make an informed pricing decision.

If there's any uncertainty as to the price, you're well advised to get an independent appraisal. For example, you may choose an agent who you think is really good, but their assessment of value and yours are quite different. If the agent says $700 000 and you think it's $720 000, you don't really need a valuer. But if there's a big gap between your expectation and your preferred agent's expectation, or if you've spoken to three or four agents and they've given you a wide range of prices, it's probably a good opportunity to get a valuer.

THE HOPEFUL PRICE

One of the great mistakes vendors can make is putting an inflated price – a hopeful price – on their property in the hope that someone might pay it. They believe they're doing the sale and themselves a service by creating the opportunity to get an outstanding price. If no one makes an offer at the hopeful price, they can always bring the price down, the vendor reasons.

A vendor might have their home valued at $825 000, but they say 'Let's try it at $900 000 and if we can't get it after a month or two, we'll reduce the price'. Now, the challenge here is that after a month or two buyer interest is reduced to a trickle. Most of the buyers who might have paid $825 000 have moved on. Once the home has remained unsold for a few months, people start to think there's something wrong with it.

For every one instance of a private treaty vendor selling for a phenomenal price, I hear a dozen stories of vendors who reject good offers, only to accept a lesser amount 12 months later. You have to accept that the market sets the price. You can influence the price by presentation and marketing, but it's rare to lift it to a whole new level.

The best house with the wrong price

If the price is wrong, even the best home in Australia can sit there unsold for ages. Rona, in Sydney's harbourside Bellevue Hill, is a 45-room, 1883 mansion and arguably one of Australia's finest houses. It sold at the end of 2004 for about $20 million, after having been on the market for around 18 months.

When it was put up for sale, the agent put out a PR piece suggesting Rona would go for $30 million or more. A lot of genuine buyers assessed that to be well above the mark. The general consensus was that it was worth about $25 million. So the PR ended up scaring a lot of people off.

At $30 million, the buyer interest was minimal and the sale dragged on and on. When a home takes more than a few months to sell, the rumours start. Everyone wants to know what's wrong with it. People start focussing on all the negatives to do with the property.

A lot of negative perceptions developed in the marketplace. Rather than people saying, 'Wow, look at that magnificent home!' they were saying, 'They're not being realistic – it's way overpriced'. I think it ended up selling for $3 to 4 million less than it should have, and that's not taking into account the opportunity costs and the amount spent on marketing.

BUYERS' WAVE

There's a phenomenon in selling real estate that I call the buyers' wave. What I've found is that the first three to four weeks that a home is on the market is when you get the maximum amount of buyer interest. Think about it … unless they've started looking this week, buyers are mainly on the lookout for *new* listings. After a few weeks on the home hunt, they've probably seen most of the suitable properties in their preferred areas and price range. So when a new property hits the market, there's a great flurry of buyer activity, with lots of people attending inspections.

BUYERS' WAVE

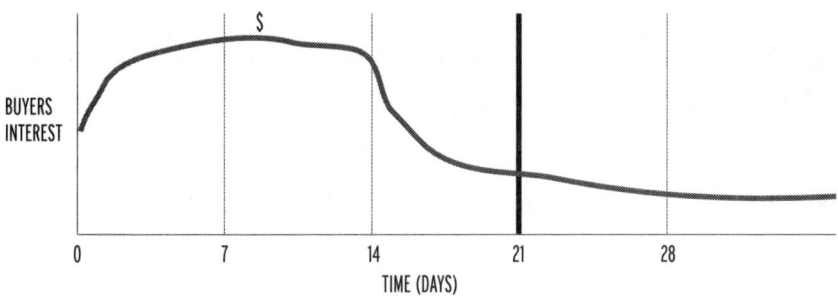

If they like the home, buyers will express some interest, otherwise they'll move on to other listings. After four weeks, buyer interest tends to tail off quite dramatically. Once a property has been on the market for more than a couple of months, you'll be lucky to get a trickle of buyers through. So it's crucial to get the pricing right during the first four weeks of the marketing campaign. If the sale is by auction, it's even more critical, because you have a limited period in which to establish qualified buyer interest.

Different prices

✳ **Ecstatic price** – beyond your wildest dreams (usually only achieved at auction).

✳ **Hopeful price** – an overly optimistic asking or reserve price. Good luck!

✳ **Asking price** – the starting point for negotiations.

✳ **Walk-away price** – the lowest amount you'll accept. This is what you set the reserve at for an auction.

✳ **Market price** – what a buyer is ready, willing and able to pay. Hopefully more than your walk-away price.

✳ **Giveaway price** – great for buyers, but bad news for vendors.

Peak enthusiasm

At the start of the marketing campaign, you and your agent are at your peak enthusiasm. You're presenting the home like the Palace of Versailles on every inspection day. You're excited and optimistic about the process, and the agent is revved up too. Buyers are flocking to the inspections and interest is good. This is the best time to sell your property – when the energy is high.

In my experience, you can't maintain highly focussed energy on the sale of a property for much longer than a month or two. And I'm not just talking about the agents – I'm talking about vendors too. Vendors get sick of buyers traipsing through and having to keep the home clean for inspections. It can be a frustrating and stressful experience if the sale drags on and on.

NEGOTIATION BUFFER

While it's important not to overprice your home, you should include a small buffer for negotiation in the price. Buyers expect to haggle a bit. Your asking price will be treated by buyers as a starting point for negotiations, not the final price. So it's sensible to list the home with a price slightly above what you expect to sell it at.

A reasonable negotiation buffer would be around 5 per cent. So if you're expecting $800000 and you list it at $840000, that's OK. But if you list it at $880000, you're going to get different buyers through, and that could cause problems.

MARKET FEEDBACK

If you've done your comparable sales research, you should have a good idea of the price you can expect, but you can never know how current buyers will value your home. Once the inspections begin, your agent can talk to buyers and get their opinion on your property. The agent will use this market feedback to make an assessment of the level of interest in your property.

A good agent will quiz buyers at inspections. They'll ask:

* What do you like/dislike about this home?

* What other comparable homes have you seen?

* Are you interested in buying this home?

* If not, why not?

* How much do you think this home is worth?

Even if they don't want to buy your home, buyers' feedback is invaluable for checking whether your pricing is right. The buyers will have been inspecting similar properties for weeks, and at the end of the day it's their opinion on price that counts.

The market is extremely efficient

It's very hard to outsmart the market, because buyers do far more research in a defined price range than vendors and agents ever can. You need to accept that, and keep your asking price or reserve in line with the market. Otherwise the only thing you're going to do is help every other vendor sell their property by making their home look like good value compared to yours.

Sometimes buyers' negative feedback relates to something you can modify during the sale process. If a lot of buyers really aren't keen on your colour scheme, window coverings or light fittings, you can do a quick upgrade. But if the most common stumbling block is the price, be prepared to adjust your expectations to accommodate market feedback.

Don't sugar-coat it

In a good agent–vendor relationship there's a free flow of information about market feedback. When I was selling, I used to ring my vendors every day. I would have a face-to-face meeting with them once a week, and I'd give them a detailed written summary of everyone who'd seen the property, all their comments and price estimates, whether they were interested or not and why they made those comments.

I prefer not to sugar-coat the feedback. Some agents prefer to tell you only the wonderful adjectives and all the positive things buyers said. I think that's misleading. I'd always ask the vendors if they were OK with me telling them everything the buyers are saying. I don't think I've ever had a vendor in 22 years who said, 'Oh no, I want you to sugar-coat it'. But the reality is that most agents do gild the lily. They want the vendor to think everyone loves their home.

Not every buyer will love your home, but you're doing yourself a disservice if you don't hear a full range of commentary about the property. Because the purpose of market feedback is to give the vendor sufficient accurate information so they can make an intelligent decision about the auction reserve or adjust the asking price if necessary.

GETTING A PREMIUM PRICE

The key to extracting a premium price for a property – in any location, at any time, in any market – is emotionally connecting a number of buyers to the home and creating competition between them. I know from my selling career that the minute I sensed a buyer had mentally moved into the home, I could expect their best offer to come forward and a deal to be done.

Eager buyers get a look in their eyes when they inspect a property. They're looking around the room and they're imagining where all their furniture is going to be. They start talking to their partners about possible renovations. 'If we knock this wall out we could put double doors in here and ...'

All of a sudden, in their mind's eye, they've already moved in. They're starting to fall in love with the property and they can see themselves and their family living there. They're visualising their future in the home. Their desire to own the home is great – they've got to have it. So, as a vendor, your goal is to get two or more buyers into this emotional state.

You can't change the location of property, the aspect, views, size or layout. So the only way to improve your chances of buyers falling in love with your home is by superior presentation. If you make the appearance of your home irresistible, buyers will perceive it as a better product and be willing to pay more.

MAKING THE SALE

The two most popular methods of selling property are by auction and private treaty. Amongst real estate experts there are strong advocates for both methods. Some say the competitive atmosphere of an auction guarantees the best price for your property. Others warn that auctions are fraught with danger, and a private treaty sale is the most effective way to wring every last dollar out of a buyer.

THE BEST METHOD OF SALE

While there are merits to both points of view, I don't believe there is one generic best way of selling. What will work best depends on a number of factors which are unique to each vendor. You'll have to do a self inventory to see which method of sale suits you best.

Are you a confident person who can handle the stresses and high emotions of an auction? Or are you a more timid and private person who would prefer a more relaxed and discreet private treaty sale? Is your property unique in some way or otherwise hard to put a value on? If so, you're probably better advised to go to auction.

What is your current financial situation? Are you in need of some quick cash? The quick turnaround of an auction will be just the ticket. Or are you just dipping your toe in the water to see if someone will make you an offer you can't refuse? Then private treaty is the way to go. Also, what amount can you budget to set aside for marketing? Finally, you need to consider the current market conditions and the level of demand for your style of property.

SELLING AT AUCTION

An auction is a public sale by a licensed auctioneer where a property is sold to the highest bidder. The vendor puts a reserve price on the property and it will not be sold until bidding has exceeded this price. If the bidding doesn't reach the reserve, the property is passed in and the highest bidder has the first right to negotiate with the vendor.

Clearly what you need for an auction to be successful is more than one bidder who is excited about your property and wants to buy it at the time of the auction. So you need to have a sense of the current market conditions, and you definitely want to have a feel for the level of demand for your type of property.

For in-demand property or for strong markets where there's a reasonable expectation that you can generate more than one buyer to compete for a property at a similar level, auction comes into its own.

Competitive bidding

Auctions are often highly emotionally charged events. It's hard for buyers to stay detached at auctions, because they've often formed an emotional attachment to the property. This attachment can range from mild, for an investor who's only interested in buying the property if they can get it at the right price, to extreme, for a home buyer who's fallen in love with the property and must have it at any price.

Several people will bid for the property, but only one will be the new owner. This competition heightens buyers' emotions and their desire to 'win'. When someone else wants what we want, we often want it twice as badly. So, all of a sudden, the buyers' attention is on winning the auction rather than on the sale price.

How high can you go?

In a private treaty sale, a buyer will ask, 'What's the price?' The agent tells them '$650 000'. The buyer's immediate thought is, 'I wonder how much below that I can get it for?' Buyers know that vendors put a margin for negotiation in the asking price. So the buyer starts thinking, 'I wonder how much negotiation room they've plugged in? Maybe I can get it for $620 000 or $600 000. Maybe they'll take $580 000 if they're desperate'.

In an auction sale, the buyers' thought process is quite different. The agent will give them a price guide, but if they've fallen in love with the property, buyers will often start thinking how much more they're prepared to pay to own the property. 'The agent says around $650 000 – I wonder how much more I would have to pay to make it mine?'

In the heat of the moment, auction bidders will often be thinking, 'How much would I go to if I had to, if I'm pushed?' All of a sudden they're thinking, 'If I had to, would I go to $670 000 or $680 000? If someone else really wants it, could I go to $700 000 because I really love this place and I don't want to miss it?'

Hard-to-value property

If a property is unique or extremely hard to value, an auction is usually the best way of determining the fair market value. Rather than the agent and vendor guessing how much the property is worth, you should simply let the market decide.

For example, you're the owner of a converted inner-city church. If it's sold by private treaty and it's overvalued or undervalued, either way is going to be a bad news result. If it's undervalued, the church sells at the first inspection and that buyer auctions it in six months' time and gets another $100 000. That's a hard pill to swallow. If you overvalue it, the property sits on the market for 12 months. All your plans are thrown out, the listing ends up going stale and you end up selling for less than you wanted.

Auction benefits

One of the advantages of an auction is that you're working to a fixed timetable. Most people don't want to stay on the market forever. They come onto the market for a specific reason and they like to move on within a reasonable time frame. And there's a reasonably good chance they're going to get a result on auction day, if not before. A fixed time frame also motivates buyers to act quickly and adds to the competitive environment.

If there is any need for probity in the sale (e.g. divorces, mortgagee sales, deceased estates or one joint owner buying the other out), auction is the best selling method. The auction process ensures that everyone has a fair opportunity to buy the property. It can never be argued after the event that the home was undersold to a friend of a friend.

Not for everyone

In my opinion, auctions are more stressful than private treaty sales because the whole selling program is condensed into a 30-day period, culminating in a one-off auction event. The vendor is required to make a decision about the reserve price before, if not during, the auction.

For some people, that stress is just too much to bear. I've come across situations where the house suited auction, but the vendor didn't. If someone's a bit frail or nervous, I would say to them, 'I wouldn't auction your home because I don't want that pressure on you'. So you definitely need to consider your disposition and how you handle stress before you choose to auction your property.

Another aspect of auctions that some vendors are uncomfortable with is the public nature of the sale. Some vendors don't really want everyone knowing how much they received for the sale of their home. If that's the case, a private treaty sale is much more discreet.

Auctioneers

If you decide to auction your home, I'd check out the auctioneer your agent uses. I believe a great auctioneer can be worth $20 000 to most vendors at the business end of an auction. Ask the agent who the auctioneer for your property would be if you chose their company, and get a list of their upcoming auctions. Then you can go and observe the auctioneer in action.

Most companies have one or two auctioneers they use, so you often don't have much leeway. For me, a bad auctioneer would be a deal breaker, because I believe the auctioneer on the day is a critical part of getting a premium. If they were just an OK auctioneer, not necessarily the best, but you had a really great feeling about the agent, I would probably go with that team. Just keep in mind that the auctioneer is an incredibly important asset.

SETTING THE RESERVE PRICE

The reserve price is usually set on auction day or the day before. The figure is confidential between you, the agent and the auctioneer. You set the reserve in consultation with your agent, so take your time to go over your comparable sales data and all the market feedback you've received. A good reserve should be an acceptable walk-away price for you, and appear achievable based on market feedback.

Let's say you set your reserve at $400 000. If the bidding exceeds that figure, you're home and hosed. However, if the bidding stalls at $380 000, you have a couple of options. Typically, the agent will give you the opportunity to lower your reserve to the highest bid. If you do this, the auctioneer will call the property on the market.

Announcing that the property is on the market is often a catalyst for further bidding. The underbidder might be on $375 000 and their partner digs them in the ribs and says, 'Let's not lose this for $10 000'. So they make another bid. Auctions often get a second wind once the auctioneer says the property is on the market.

But, as a vendor, you have to consider your position carefully. Because, just as easily, the bidding could finish then and there and you'd have to sell at that price. If you decide not to lower your reserve, the agent will usually ask the highest bidder if they want to raise their bid. If they choose to meet the reserve, the property is called on the market. Further bidding may ensue.

Your final option is to pass the property in. The highest bidder usually has the right to negotiate with you first, and will often buy the property straight after the auction. If the auction's been properly conducted and the property was priced right, there's usually not a huge gap between the highest bid and the reserve.

WHAT IF IT'S PASSED IN?

One of a vendor's biggest fears is that their property will be passed in on auction day. With auction clearance rates usually ranging from 35 to 85 per cent, this is a very real risk. But it's important to remember that the auction is not the be-all and end-all of the selling process. In fact, there are several opportunities for a property to be sold in an auction campaign. The property can be sold prior to auction, on auction day under the hammer, on auction day after it's been passed in, or in the days after the auction if it's not sold on the day.

After having sold thousands of properties at auction, obviously I've had to pass in a number of those. But I've never found selling a property to be an issue after auction. From my experience, most properties passed in at auction usually sell by private treaty within 14 days. The auction unearths the best buyers in the market at that point in time, and a good agent will negotiate over the next few days with one of those buyers. If the vendor is realistic about their price expectations, they can hope to sell promptly.

Low or no bids

Some vendors are uncomfortable with auctions because they believe that if their property is passed in at a low price, it will create a bad impression with buyers and make it hard to sell. I don't agree with that, because the vendor has some influence on the passed-in bid.

You have the right to make a vendor bid at the auction, so you can place that bid at a price you're comfortable with. Or, if there's no bidding, you have the choice to 'no bid' the auction or place a vendor bid and pass in the auction on your vendor bid.

The buyers who don't buy your property at auction go onto something else. Fresh buyers are coming into the market every week. So if you pass in your property on your vendor bid, you give them a clear indication of your price.

SELLING BY PRIVATE TREATY

Compared to the theatre of a public auction, a sale by private treaty is a less dramatic and more discreet selling process. Thus it appeals to vendors who are too timid for auction or who like to keep their affairs private. It can also be a cheaper option than auction.

The whole purpose of an auction is to create sufficient buyer interest to create a competitive bidding situation. Now, there's no point having an auction if you're going to keep it a secret. It's imperative to do an effective marketing campaign to reach the maximum number of potential buyers in the allotted time. (With an auction you also pay for the auctioneer and the auction venue if it's off-site.)

Whereas with a private treaty sale, you may not have to invest any money in marketing at all. For example, your agent may find someone to buy your home from their database of buyers. For this reason, private treaty gives a vendor an excellent opportunity to dip their toe in the water without making a significant investment in marketing.

If you'd consider selling if a buyer offers what you think is the right price, but you don't want to invest 1 per cent of the property's value to try to find that out, then private treaty is a good choice for you.

Private treaty benefits

A private treaty sale allows you time to consider offers by potential buyers. So it's a less stressful process than an auction, where vendors are often called on to make snap decisions on auction day.

Because there's no fixed timetable for the sale, you can extend the sale of your home indefinitely. This is a bonus if you can afford to wait until someone offers you the price you want, but a big drawback if you want a quick turnaround. Few vendors relish the prospect of their homes languishing on the market for more than eight weeks. I've known vendors who have had their property on the market for 12 months. That's not going to suit most people.

NEGOTIATING WITH BUYERS

The best negotiation advice I can give vendors is the same advice I give buyers: care, but not that much. The best negotiators I've come across are able to slightly detach themselves from the process. They don't get too emotionally involved. They're typically very well researched and remain quite calm.

From a vendor's perspective, you don't want to put yourself under extreme pressure in the negotiations. Ideally you want to be in a position where you don't have to sell unless you achieve a price that you're comfortable with.

So I always recommend to my clients to sell their home before buying another. Because if you've already bought a new home, you're very attached to the result of any negotiation. It's very hard not to care that much when you've got a bridging-finance interest bill ticking over. If you have to make a deal to a deadline, the time pressure can work against you in the negotiation.

If you sell your home first, the worst-case scenario is that you may have to rent a home for a short period. If you buy first, the worst-case scenario is not selling your first home, ending up with two mortgages, bridging finance and potentially losing both properties. Neither scenario is perfect, but I'd much prefer to rent a home for six months than have to pay two mortgages.

How much do you want?

The negotiation process begins before you start receiving offers from buyers. It actually starts with the research you've done to set your asking price. You should have done sufficient research so that you're comfortable and satisfied that the price you're aiming for is achievable. When you're realistic about your price and have a good grasp on current market values, you can negotiate a lot harder in that knowledge.

Before you start negotiating, you should define what you want. Otherwise how will you know if your negotiations have been successful? What is the price you want and what is the minimum you'll accept – your walk-away price?

Your negotiations are influenced by a mixture of hope and realism. You're hoping someone will pay your asking price, but realistically you may have to accept less. Your asking price is only the starting point for the negotiations. The offers that buyers submit are the reality of how the market values your property.

Stay flexible

The offers are the market. If you've done sufficient research on comparable prices, and set your asking price accordingly, you can expect that serious offers should be within a reasonable negotiating range of your walk-away price. And this is the case most of the time.

But no matter how comprehensive your comparable sales analysis has been, you can never know how much buyers will offer. One cheeky offer can be seen in isolation. But if you receive five offers substantially lower than your asking price, you have to consider whether that's the fair market value of your home.

It can be a mistake to take an unyielding position of 'I won't accept one dollar less for my home, no matter what happens'. I'm not suggesting you accept any low-ball offer that comes along. But you have to consider all offers with an open mind.

Market shifts

Perhaps your expectations were overly optimistic, or perhaps the market has shifted since you listed. You need to keep in touch with the market during your sale, because information is a very important negotiation tool and, typically, the person with the best information will often end up succeeding.

Talk to your agent and see what else has hit the market since you listed your property for sale. Have any comparable properties sold recently? Subtle fluctuations in the local market will influence how buyers value your home. If a similar home in your neighbourhood sold for less than your asking price, it could make your place seen overpriced. Conversely, a premium price paid for a comparable property may make your home appear good value.

WORKING WITH YOUR AGENT

Typically your agent will be doing the face-to-face negotiations on your behalf. If you've selected your agent carefully, you will have chosen a competent negotiator who will always negotiate with your best interests in mind. A good agent will negotiate to maximise your price and won't try to persuade you to accept just any offer.

During negotiations, the agent's role is to justify your price to the buyers. For example, if I was selling a home for $600 000 and a buyer offered $550 000, I would ask them, 'How did you arrive at that figure?' I want to know what they're thinking and what comparables they've used to come up with their offer, because they might be using incorrect comparables.

So, if the buyer says, 'Well, a similar home down the road sold for $550 000', I can say, 'Well, actually, I've got the Registrar General's records which say it actually sold for $575 000. I agree it's reasonably comparable, but this house has a garage, and in this area a garage has got to be worth around $25 000 or $30 000, which brings us back to the asking price'.

ARE THEY SERIOUS?

An owner-occupier will rarely make an offer on a property that they're not very keen to own. Making an offer is clear evidence of the buyer's emotional connection to the property. By the time the buyer gets to the negotiation table, they've mentally moved into the home. (Property investors are in a slightly different situation, because typically they have multiple options and they're less emotionally connected.)

So if you receive a sensible offer, you can negotiate with confidence. Nonetheless, you still need to gauge just how keen the buyer is. You need to assess the offer for its strong and weak points, and to judge just how serious the buyer is.

When an offer is made, a good agent will find out all the details surrounding the offer. Have the buyers got their finance approved? Is the offer written or verbal? Have the buyers signed a contract? What are their terms of the offer? Are they offering a 5 per cent or 10 per cent deposit, or a deposit bond? Do they want a 6-week or 12-week settlement? What inclusions do they expect?

Get it in writing

A serious buyer will make a serious offer to indicate their intention to own your home. As a vendor, and as a vendor's agent, I always want to get the offer in writing. A verbal offer can come and go very quickly. A written offer shows that the buyer is keen. A signed contract, especially if it has a deposit cheque attached, demonstrates that the buyer is highly motivated.

ASSESSING THE OFFER

After all the effort you've put into working with your agent and preparing your home for sale, it's a relief when the offers start rolling in. But it's not unusual for vendors to be a little underwhelmed by the offers they receive – especially at the early stages of negotiation.

Rarely do buyers offer full price, and if the market's cold, their first offer may be substantially below your asking price. And if the market's red hot and you do get offered your asking price, you might be plagued by doubts that you've undersold the property and that you could get more.

Before you get carried away by your emotions, make an objective assessment of the offer to gauge its merits. There are several factors you need to assess before you decide on your next move:

Price

How much is the buyer offering? Have they given any justification for the price offered, such as recent comparable sales?

Deposit

How much deposit are they offering? Will the deposit be cash or a deposit bond? Have they included a cheque for the deposit amount?

Terms and conditions

What settlement period, inclusions and occupancy are they suggesting?

Subject-to offers

Are there any contingency clauses (e.g. subject to suitable finance) that weaken the offer?

Once you've assessed the strong and weak points of the offer, you can decide to accept or reject the offer, or make a counteroffer.

WIN-WIN NEGOTIATIONS

Negotiating is a normal part of the selling process that buyers expect to participate in. Even if your property is priced spot-on the fair market value, a buyer will still want to negotiate. They want to feel like they've got a good deal. That's why it's important to add a reasonable negotiation buffer to your walk-away price to allow a little bit of room for bargaining.

The negotiations are really about perceived value. If a buyer perceives that they're getting good value and that they have negotiated a fair outcome for themselves, they're far more likely to go ahead with the sale. That's why it's important to always treat buyers with respect and allow them some concessions, so they feel like they've had a win.

Concessions and trade-offs

Price isn't the only element of negotiation in a property sale. There are multiple concessions that can be negotiated other than price, such as the length of settlement, certain inclusions such as light fittings, curtains or a dishwasher, or early occupancy. Terms and conditions are the most flexible negotiation element to add (or subtract) value to the deal.

During the negotiation process, be mindful of all the elements, not just the price, and be prepared to make some trade-offs to clinch the deal. For example, if someone's still got to sell their own property before they buy yours, rather than lower your price you could give them a three- to six-month settlement. This gives the buyer leeway to sell their property first, saving them the expense and hassle of bridging finance.

Lowball offers

Buyers will often test the waters with an initial offer much lower than your asking price. They'll put forward a lowball offer to see where your head is at. Property investors often take the attitude 'nothing ventured, nothing gained' and put out lowball offers in the hope of buying a bargain.

Don't feel compelled to counter a lowball offer. You can reject the offer, but be mindful not to offend the buyer, because you want to keep them at the negotiation table. By rejecting the lowball offer, you can give a very clear message that the home is for sale at a fair price, but not at a bargain price.

The way you handle the rejection is quite important, because you don't want to offend the buyer. You can communicate through your agent that you appreciate the buyer's interest. Thank them for the offer, but let them know it's not acceptable. Keep it pleasant but firm.

But you said ...

Make sure you confirm all the details of the offer upfront. Negotiations sometimes fall over at the eleventh hour because the parties couldn't agree on some minor terms. I've seen a half-million dollar sale come apart over a dishwasher that was worth $500. Suddenly the deal becomes a battle of egos.

FINDING YOUR BUYER

Keep in mind that not every buyer is your buyer. You have to be prepared to walk away from a few buyers if they're not willing to meet your price, especially if they're tyre kickers or bargain hunters. If the cheeky offer is just a 'try-on', the buyer will either move on to another property or, if they genuinely want to buy your home, they'll make another offer.

If their cheeky offer is rejected, a genuine buyer will ask the agent, 'Well, what is an acceptable offer?' A good agent will tell them, 'The asking price is acceptable, and we think it's a fair price based on these facts ...' All of a sudden the buyer will come up and make an offer which is closer to your asking price.

Negotiating is a bit like chess – your initial move depends on the buyer's initial move. Rejecting a cheeky offer is a strategic move –

you're calling the buyer's bluff. When you receive an offer that's in the ballpark of your walk-away price, with terms and conditions within acceptable parameters, the negotiations can begin in earnest.

KEEPING THE MOMENTUM

Your goal is to narrow the gap between the buyer's offer and your asking price. You keep up the momentum of the negotiations by making counteroffers. You never know what buyers are thinking, so by making a counteroffer you begin to flush out the buyer's best offer.

If you've chosen a good agent, you can trust them to negotiate the best price and terms and conditions on your behalf. At this point, you need to have a high degree of confidence in your agent and their recommendations.

Start by looking at the terms and conditions. What does the buyer need to help them close the deal? Can you trade off a higher price for terms that are favourable to the buyer? Be prepared to give a few concessions, because if you hold out for every last penny and every favourable term, you can risk losing what otherwise may be a great deal.

WHEN TO ACCEPT AN OFFER

Before you accept an offer, there are a few factors you have to weigh up. You need to do a reality check on your asking price and how you arrived at it. How realistic is it? Then assess the market feedback between when you put the property on the market and the offer. Finally, what is the average number of days on market? If it's 30 days and your home's been on the market for 60 days, that could be a sign that it's time to start looking at sensible offers.

Vendors are often weighing up, 'How much do I have to get to make the next move?' That's not really a good basis for deciding to take an offer or not. It's an important consideration for you, but buyers are not going to be swayed by the fact that you're moving to a better area and you need to get another $50 000 to make it work. Buyers make offers based on comparable sales.

When it comes to weighing up offers, a good agent will come into their own – they'll guide you. I've often received what the vendors thought was an acceptable offer in the first week, but I've recommended not accepting. If I believe the buyer will go higher, or there's serious interest from other parties, I'll recommend the vendor wait a little bit longer.

If you've chosen the right agent, they won't let you undersell your home. They'll make sure you hang in there until you get the best price.

Offers don't last for ever

By the time a buyer puts in an offer for a home, they're really excited about owning it. But in the face of rejection or procrastination by the vendor their enthusiasm can quickly fade. They'll often start talking themselves out of it. So it's a good idea to respond to any offers promptly.

WHY HOMES DON'T SELL

There are only three reasons a property doesn't sell – price, presentation and marketing. If the price is wrong, you can have a booming market and superb presentation, but the property can sit unsold for 12 months. If it's poorly presented but well priced, it will still sell, but there's definitely a positive emotional impact of having a well-presented home that looks and feels right.

And marketing? Well, if you don't get the right buyer to the doorstep of the property, then you're not going to sell it. So if your home is well presented and well priced but you haven't stimulated enough buyer interest, again, it's going to sit around. So you should put your efforts into pricing the home well, making an excellent presentation and ensuring you have a good marketing program.

What happened?

If your property isn't selling, you need to take stock of what's gone wrong. Sit down with your agent and have a look at the variables. Was the presentation up to scratch? Did you achieve sufficient coverage with your marketing? Was your asking price realistic?

From my experience, price is the culprit in 80 per cent of failed sales. Because by the time most vendors get their property on the market, it's presented as well as it's ever going to be. And they usually have an adequate marketing program, especially if it was an auction sale.

So you'll need to ask yourself whether the asking price was too optimistic. What were the offers that came in? Often a vendor will be a bit scathing when an offer comes in. Perhaps they're expecting $600 000, and someone offers $540 000. They're disappointed and perhaps a little anxious. But if no one else has made an offer they might want to start considering whether $540 000 is really what the home is worth.

Did the agent perform?

You should also look at your agent's performance. Has your agent done everything possible? Did they fulfil all their promises? Do you feel they represented your property with enthusiasm, energy and integrity? Don't be too hasty to blame the agent though, because they're paid by commission, so every single day they're focussed on getting a result that works for you. But if you've lost faith in your agent or they didn't deliver on their promises, it's probably time to move on.

GOING FORWARD

Once you and the agent have debriefed, you can consider the options for going forward. But before you commit to doing anything, it's a good idea to pause for a breather, because you're probably a bit flat and have lost momentum. You need to recover your positive energy, or your lack of enthusiasm can negatively impact the sale. I've found taking the home off the market for a few weeks is sometimes quite effective.

If your pricing has been out of whack, you can continue the sale via private treaty with your new asking price, or you can go to auction. Vendors who have already had their home passed in at auction may be reluctant to go through the experience again. But I've actually had huge success re-auctioning properties.

One of my colleagues, Mark McLeod, a real estate sales trainer from Queensland, claims that 95 per cent of re-auctions result in a sale. This is because, after the first auction, vendors now understand where the market value is at, and they tend to readjust their reserve price accordingly.

If you employ a new agent, you can make a fresh start with a new set of sales collateral. If you've been to auction, you should own all of the sales collateral, such as the pictures, floor plan and the copy. Ask your agent to return these to you. You could try repositioning your home, creating new collateral using your existing pictures and fresh copy.

Seasons change

If your home hasn't sold, you should consider the seasonal fluctuations in market activity. Some times of the year – such as spring and early summer – traditionally have more sales activity than others. If you auctioned your home in autumn and it didn't sell, you might want to take it off the market for a month or two over the winter period and re-present it in spring. There are natural punctuation points in the market seasons that you can align your sale with.

INVESTING

WHY INVEST IN PROPERTY?

In my opinion, well-located, actively managed investment property is one of the best investments for everyday investors. With an attractive combination of solid capital growth, regular income and generous tax breaks, it's a simple investment that most people can understand. With a little effort and know-how, you can convert a modest deposit into a sizable nest egg.

MY FIRST PROPERTY INVESTMENT

In 1984 I bought a little fixer-upper terrace in Hargrave Street, Paddington, in Sydney. Nowadays, Paddington is blue-ribbon real estate, but back then the suburb was quite run-down and bohemian. I paid $96 000 for the terrace and it was pretty much uninhabitable.

I got together with a few friends and we knocked it into shape so I could put some tenants in. Their rent basically covered the majority of the mortgage payments, and I put in a little bit more cash to make up the shortfall. Paddington prices were on the way up, so I started enjoying capital growth from day one.

A couple of years later I bought a two-bedroom apartment in Cook Road, Centennial Park, for $105 000. Since I had bought the terrace, the market had gone up and its value had increased. I borrowed against the increased equity in the terrace for a deposit, so now I had secured two properties.

A few years later, when I started my real estate agency, I needed capital, so unfortunately I had to sell those properties. I sold the terrace for $260 000 and the unit for $240 000. So from the original acquisition cost of $201 000, capital growth had increased the value of the properties to $500 000. Needless to say, I was thrilled.

Later on, I was telling my accountant about how great my first experience in property investment had been, turning $201 000 into $500 000. He pointed out that since I'd only put down a $10 000 deposit on each property, I'd actually turned $20 000 of my own cash into a $299 000 capital gain.

Some good advice

I started selling real estate when I was 20 and my first boss, John O'Brien, gave me some really good advice. He said, 'Live within your means, save as much you can and buy property as soon as you can afford it'. I was paid a small base salary and a commission. So I lived frugally on my salary and put all my commissions into a bank account until I'd saved enough money for a small deposit.

THE POWER OF LEVERAGE

This story is a great example of the power of leverage. The basic principle of leverage is borrowing money to buy an appreciating asset. If the asset goes up in value faster than the amount you have to repay, your wealth increases. Leverage is a way to increase your gains by investing with borrowed funds.

For example, consider two investors who each have $100 000 to spend. Investor One pays cash for a property worth $100 000. Investor Two uses the $100 000 as a deposit and buys a property worth $500 000, borrowing the remaining $400 000. If property values go up 10 per cent annually, Investor One makes $10 000 in the first year, but Investor Two makes $50 000.

Consider their position after 10 years:

Year	Investor One	Investor Two
	Value of property	
0	100 000	500 000
1	110 000	550 000
2	121 000	605 000
3	133 100	665 500
4	146 410	732 050
5	161 051	805 255
6	177 156	885 781
7	194 872	974 359
8	214 359	1 071 794
9	235 795	1 178 974
10	259 374	1 296 871
Less debt	0	-400 000
Equity	**259 374**	**896 871**

By using leverage to buy more real estate, Investor Two ends up with more than three times the amount of equity as Investor One.

Of course it's not quite as simple as that. I haven't taken into account such factors as rental income, interest payments or tax. But the purpose of my example is to demonstrate that borrowing money enables Investor Two to control more assets and thus make more profit.

Safe as houses

The reason why property is so attractive is because it has better leverage than almost all other types of investments. Most lenders prefer financing property as opposed to other investments because it's much less risky. It's tangible, prices don't fluctuate wildly, and it's easy to value.

On the other hand, business is considered a high-risk investment because businesses go broke all the time. Consequently, lenders are cautious about lending money to invest in business or buy shares.

But banks and other lenders are very keen to lend you money to buy property. In fact, you'll see their ads encouraging you to do so almost every time you open the newspaper or turn on your TV. Property is considered a safe and secure investment, and it's the preferred security for lenders.

You can control a significant piece of real estate with a relatively modest amount of capital. Lenders may be willing to lend you 50 per cent of the value of blue-chip stocks. But they'll happily lend you 80, 90 or even 100 per cent or more of the value of a property.

SIGNIFICANT ADVANTAGES

Property's leverage advantage can enable you to build your wealth faster than many other forms of investment. Residential property also has seven other significant advantages which I believe make it an excellent investment for the average Australian.

1. You can add value

Property is one of the few investments that you can easily add value to. Over a few weekends with a few friends who were in the building trade, I transformed a derelict terrace into an income-producing asset. I increased the value of the property and the rental income for very little outlay.

There are literally hundreds of ways to add value to a property, many of which cost only a small amount of money. You can paint it, build a barbecue, put in some paving, hang new curtains, replace the benchtops, steam clean the carpets, modernise the light fittings, replace all the doorknobs … the list goes on and on. You're only limited by your imagination.

2. Consistent growth

On average, over the past 100 years, Australia property had a growth of around 10 per cent per annum. That means home prices doubled every 7 to 10 years.

3. You can access your profits without selling

If your property goes up in value, you don't have to sell it to access your profit. You simply refinance. You get a new valuation of the property and borrow more funds using the increased equity as security.

4. Exceptional tax advantages

Property offers excellent tax advantages through negative gearing, which allows you to offset any losses against your other income. Always get advice from an accountant to maximise the tax benefits from your property investment. The amount you pay them will be recouped many times over by the amount of tax they save you.

5. The property market is relatively stable and predictable

The growth trends in property are much less volatile than many other forms of investment, with fewer variations from the average. If 49 houses in a street have increased in value by 10 per cent, then it's highly likely the fiftieth house in the street has also gone up by 10 per cent. Property values in a given area tend to move in unison.

Fluctuations in the property market typically occur over a much longer period. Property is not that easy to dispose of, which discourages panic selling. Also, 67 per cent of property in Australia is owner-occupied, which provides another buffer against fluctuations.

If you pick up the paper and it says 'Property market off the boil', you don't sell your home, because you still need somewhere to live. You can't live in shares. People tend to stay put in tougher times. They'll delay their plans to sell until they feel the time is right, and continue to enjoy their home in the meantime.

6. Easy to understand

After 20 years of investing in the stock market, I still don't really understand very much about shares. Whereas property is a tangible asset that's very easy for most people to research and understand.

People feel comfortable investing in residential property. They have a good idea of how property 'works', so they don't have to learn everything from scratch or familiarise themselves with new terminology.

7.   Combines growth and income with low risk

There are three factors you have to weigh up in any investment: growth, income and risk. Well-located residential property is one of the few investments that offer both substantial income and capital growth, all with a low risk.

MY INVESTMENT STRATEGY

Building wealth through property investment is a skill that can be learnt by anyone. Having read this far, you're probably three-quarters of the way there already. Once you understand the basic principles, learn the rules, develop a plan and take action, you'll be well on the way to building a profitable portfolio.

Successful property investment is more about good management than good luck. You need a simple and effective strategy to guide you. My preferred strategy focuses on maximising capital growth while keeping risk to a minimum:

Buy well-located property and hold for the long term, using the incentives of the tax system to help you pay for it.

This strategy enables you to build wealth quickly and manage your risks so you can sleep at night.

Location is the key

The old real estate adage 'location, location, location' is especially true for investment property. There's a direct relationship between location and demand, and demand is the biggest driver of capital growth. So to maximise your capital growth, you have to buy the best property in the best possible location you can afford.

It comes down to basic economics. If demand exceeds supply, prices go up. The biggest influence on demand in the property market is location. People will always prefer to live 15 minutes from the CBD rather than two hours' drive away, and they'd prefer to have the beach at their front door rather than 10 blocks away.

Location is a crucial factor, because it's the one thing you can't change once you've bought the property. Scarcity is what makes a good location great. The supply of property in good locations can't easily be increased, and as the population increases, so does the demand, forcing prices up.

Buy the best

For this investment strategy to succeed, the capital growth must exceed your contributions. You need to do your research and buy the best location you can afford.

Sleep-at-night factor

I'm a fairly conservative and risk-adverse investor. I'm not a great lover of debt. Perhaps I'd be a lot better off financially if I was. But I don't think you need to be a huge risk taker or to borrow beyond your means to create a profitable investment property portfolio, because I wasn't.

I'm an investor rather than a speculator. Lots of people make money speculating on the property market – traders, renovators, developers – but I wouldn't recommend it unless you know what you're doing. There's much less risk and less stress if you buy for the long term. I recommend holding onto your investment property for a minimum of five years, preferably longer.

Stick with it

The most common motivation for buying investment property is to secure a long-term investment. I wouldn't recommend investing in property unless you have at least a five-year horizon. However, many people sell prematurely, before they've reaped the rewards. They get bored or they can't see immediate results. So they sell and invest their money elsewhere.

If the market flattens out, don't despair. Don't feel compelled to get out and don't feel embarrassed. Just ride with it, because in two or three years' time the market will probably not only have caught up, but it will have given you a handsome profit. You need to be patient while the magic of capital growth takes effect.

Property values don't rise steadily. They tend to stay flat for a period and then surge upwards before flattening out again. Time smoothes out the effect of these fluctuations. When you invest for capital growth over the long term, the price you paid, ups and downs in interest rates and market cycles are of less consequence due to the levelling effect of time.

IDLE SPECULATION

If you want a speculative investment, I wouldn't recommend property. If you want to trade and speculate, stick with shares. They're easier, cheaper and quicker to buy and sell. The transactional costs of property are such that often the first year or two's capital growth can be absorbed in entry and exit costs.

During property booms you always hear about people making quick money. I'm not saying that's impossible. But I believe that more people lose money from trying to speculate on quick property trades. It's very hard to pick the top and the bottom of the market, and the costs are great if you get it wrong. You're better off sticking to property as a long-term wealth accumulation strategy.

TAX INCENTIVES

In essence, an investment property is a business and so, generally speaking, you're subject to the same tax obligations and perks as any other business. All the rent you collect is assessable for income tax, and all the expenses you incur running the 'business' are tax-deductible.

The major expenses for landlords are interest on money borrowed to buy the property or to make improvements, property manager's fees, insurance, maintenance, advertising and accountant's fees. All these items can be claimed as immediate tax deductions, but in order to claim them you first need to spend the cash.

But if you own a newer property, you're also entitled to claim deductions for non-cash expenses, namely depreciation. Buildings are depreciable over 40 years, so you're entitled to claim 2.5 per cent of the cost of the building as a tax deduction every year. You can claim a depreciation allowance on renovations as well.

Negative gearing

Property investment is a great way to legally minimise your tax, because you're allowed to claim a deduction for negatively geared properties. Negative gearing occurs when the costs of owning the property exceed the rental income received from it. In other words, the property is making a loss.

For taxation purposes, you can deduct this loss against income you earn from other sources such as your job or business. The result is that your taxable income is lower and thus your tax burden is lessened, but you still have to contribute cash to your investment property as long as it is negatively geared.

Of course this begs the inevitable question, 'Why would you want to invest to make a loss?' The answer is: because the capital growth of your property is greater than the cash you're putting in.

Someone earning an income of $60 000 per annum can typically purchase a $500 000 property for $100 per week after tax. If average growth is 9 per cent per annum, the property's value increases $45 000 a year. But the investor only puts in $5200, making a $39 800 net gain annually.

Why choose capital growth?

Capital growth property investment sacrifices income to some degree for superior growth, but you can claim a tax deduction on any shortfall between income and expenses. It allows you to build your wealth quickly and later in life you can convert your assets into cash.

CASH FLOW PROPERTY INVESTMENT

There is another property investment strategy that's worth mentioning. It's called cash flow, or positively geared, property investment. The essence of this strategy is that the return you make from the property exceeds the amount you pay in interest and expenses. Typically, each cash flow property returns between $30 and $100 per week, before tax.

The trick to cash flow investing is doing the numbers and finding properties with the appropriate return on investment. These properties are easier to find in regional areas where rental yields are high and capital growth low. You might have to do some renovations in order to be able to increase the rent to a level where the property is cash flow positive.

Which strategy is better? That depends on your investing goals. Cash flow property provides regular income, so you can become financially independent and quit your job if you choose. But it's a lot of work, because very few properties are suitable. You'll need to do lots of research to find them and you'll need to buy lots to replace your salary.

Capital growth property investment aims for high growth, with the consequence that you have to contribute to the costs of owning the property. Your small regular cash input – a type of saving if you like –

can lead to a big retirement nest egg in time.

If you're interested in finding out more about cash flow property investment, get a copy of *From 0 to 130 Properties in 3.5 Years* by Steve McKnight.

BUYING YOUR INVESTMENT PROPERTY

To appreciate the importance of buying in the right location, you need to understand a little bit about the underlying causes of capital growth. A basic economic principle is that if demand exceeds supply, prices will go up. That's the foundation of capital growth.

To get superior capital growth in the property market, we need to focus on demand. We don't really have to worry about supply, because in established suburbs the supply of property is relatively fixed. Blocks can be subdivided or rezoned for residential use, and houses can be knocked down and apartment blocks built in their place. But the supply doesn't increase that much.

The factor that drives property growth is demand – the greater the demand, the greater the capital growth. But what creates demand? One of the biggest influences on demand in the property market is location.

THE RIGHT LOCATION

Buying in-demand property is an essential component of my property investment strategy. Good locations will always be in demand, so you should always buy the best location you can afford. In my view, the key factors which identify a superior location are as follows.

Coffee culture and retail villages

Australian coffee consumption is about 2.4 kilograms per person per annum, double that of 30 years ago. This increase is (at least in part) due to the rise of coffee culture. Cafés, rather than pubs, are now our preferred space for meeting old friends and discussing the important issues of the day. They are an important part of our social lives.

A popular café builds a sense of community and adds great appeal to a neighbourhood. People also like the convenience of being able to shop for their necessities and life's little luxuries without going too far from home – preferably on foot. A retail village, with its cafés, delis and boutiques, often gives a suburb its unique sense of character.

Ones to watch – Perth

My predictions for good capital growth in Perth in 2005 are as follows:

* Byford
* Claremont
* Coogee/Munster/Spearwood
* Glendalough/Osborne Park
* Joondalup

* Karrinyup/Carine/Duncraig

* Rockingham

* Swan Valley

* Waterman's Bay

* Wembley

Transportation hubs

As Australia's cities get bigger, we're starting to see commuting gridlock. Most of the jobs and services are located in or near the CBD, so many people have to travel each day to work and shop. Thus, homes in close proximity to a transportation hub – be it a train station, bus or tram stop, ferry wharf or an expressway on ramp – are highly sought after. The quicker the commuting time to the CBD, the bigger the demand.

Beaches and waterways

Australians have a longstanding love affair with the ocean. Coastal regions continue to be the preferred place to live – and as close to the beach as possible. With many retiring baby boomers now seeking a sea change, it's unlikely this demand is going to wane any time soon.

Close to the CBD

As it becomes harder to get in and out of the CBD, homes within easy access to workplaces and urban amenities – such as entertainment, cafés, restaurants and medical centres – become increasingly desirable. The 'inner ring' suburbs (within 15 kilometres of the CBD) have historically provided stronger growth than suburbs further out.

Heritage precincts

In my experience, well-established suburbs with period architecture tend to grow faster than newer suburbs. People appreciate the architectural uniqueness and consistency, and often local councils have maintained the heritage character of the suburb. New homes can be duplicated and built in any number of locations, and lack the same scarcity value.

Best location within a location

Not every investor can afford to buy an inner-city terrace or a waterside home. You first have to narrow your search to suburbs that are within your budget. Then you drill down a little further and find the best position within that suburb, because each suburb usually has several different precincts, each with a different level of demand. You need to find out which streets, which side of the street and which aspect are most sought after.

FUTURE GROWTH

When it comes to good locations, some are made by God and some are made by man. Put it this way: no developer could ever recreate the beauty and grandeur of Sydney Harbour. Thus, harbourside suburbs will always be in demand because the supply of property is limited and, as the population increases, more and more people will want to live there.

However, the features that make Sydney's inner-city suburb of Paddington, or Melbourne's Carlton, so desirable – the tastefully rejuvenated heritage housing stock, cosmopolitan café society and fashionable retail precinct – could be replicated in another suburb. If that suburb was a similar distance from the CBD, you'd expect similar capital growth. And in fact that's what's happening right now in Sydney's nearby Surry Hills and Melbourne's Richmond.

My point is that locations can change from slum to blue ribbon over time. Down-at-heel working-class dormitory suburbs are transformed into charming inner-city havens. New roads and public transport links bring suburbs 'closer' to the CBD. Suburbs are rezoned, polluting factories shut down, and warehouses converted into designer apartments.

Buy now!

In 10 years' time, people will look back and marvel at how cheap property prices are now. So start right now, because it's costing you 10 per cent per annum to stay out of the market.

FINDING HOT SPOTS

Savvy property investors are always on the lookout for the hot spots of tomorrow, because that's where the greatest potential for capital growth lies. They search for the up-and-coming suburbs, on the brink of transformation by urban renewal, gentrification or improved infrastructure. The telltale signs of potential future growth locations are as follows:

Beneficial new infrastructure – new roads, public transport, schools, hospitals. But beware: some infrastructure can have a negative impact (e.g. noise and air pollution).

Urban renewal and gentrification – if the renovators are moving in en masse, it could be a good time to buy.

Redevelopment – new retail complexes and industrial sites being converted to residential. But beware: oversupply of apartments can dilute demand.

Changing lifestyle preferences – increased popularity of apartment living, café society and sea changers.

Phone a friend

Ask your friends, 'Where would you live if you could live anywhere? Where do you think are the emerging hot areas? Where do you find really interesting to go and visit?' Their answers are really good indicators of where to buy, because your peers are probably the same sort of people who will inevitably drive demand in those areas.

Courage and vision

One thing you need to realise is that to get the bigger gains, you'll often have to take a leap of faith. When people bought terraces in Paddington in the 1970s, it was a suburb in decline. It was neglected and run-down, and terraces were considered shoddy housing stock at that time. But visionary bargain hunters bought anyway, renovated and enjoyed the ride as prices skyrocketed through the eighties and nineties.

So if you're going to lead the charge, you have to be prepared to take a bit of a risk. If you were to identify the top 10 suburbs for future growth today, they'd probably be a bit daggy. They might be adjoining fashionable locations, but they probably have a mix of industrial sites and dilapidated homes, and not a whole lot of street life. I doubt you'd be able to get a decent cappuccino.

THE BIG PICTURE

One of the most important things for property investors to investigate is current demographic and lifestyle trends. Have a look at where our society is heading and work out how that will impact on housing demand and prices. Changing lifestyle preferences, the ageing of the population, the influence of the baby boomers, and the increasing financial independence of women are just some of the key trends shaping Australians' housing choices.

Baby boomers

Baby boomers are probably the most economically influential generation that we've ever seen in this country. They are, and will continue to be, the biggest influence on the property market. As the boomers start to retire en masse, they're searching for a better lifestyle. And where do these empty nesters want to live? Near the beach or near the city is the short answer.

The popularity of coastal living and demand for quality inner-city apartments is being driven by baby boomers. While their preferences will probably move towards communal living in the future, the boomers' appetite for secure, low-maintenance, lifestyle-orientated property near waterways or the CBD is here to stay for at least the next 10 years.

Ones to watch – Brisbane

My top suburbs for capital growth in Brisbane in 2005 are on the river and/or close to the CBD:

* Fairfield
* Jindalee
* Kangaroo Point
* Nundah
* Yeronga
* West End

The rise of apartments

Demand for property is shifting from established freestanding homes in the suburbs towards newer, smaller homes closer to urban amenities and lifestyle attractions. Changing lifestyle preferences and the ageing of Australia's population is reducing the size of Australian households. So while our population is growing slowly, household formation is growing at a much stronger rate.

More and more buyers, both young and old, now prefer to live in medium- and high-density developments close to the city and beaches. Smaller families, the impact of the baby boomers, and the lack of serviced land for detached housing in some cities mean that this trend will continue in the long term.

As our capital cities get bigger, there are a couple of consequences. One is commuting gridlock, where it becomes harder and harder to get in and out of the CBD. The other is the 'New York factor', as personal security becomes more of an issue. As a result, the demand for low-maintenance, well-located, secure property increases.

Developers have really upped their game in the last 10 years. They're starting to build some really high-quality, well-designed apartments that appeal to the discerning young professional and baby-boomer market.

Coastal living

Currently in Australia there's a huge sea change towards coastal living. More and more Aussies regard living by the seaside as a permanent lifestyle choice rather than just a holiday option. Homes within a short distance of beaches and waterways are very popular. So from a buying point of view, the signals are clear that property by the water or in near-coastal villages is going to have excellent capital growth over the next decade in Australia.

Single career women

Single career women are now an influential buying force in the property market. When I started in real estate, it was very rare to conduct an auction and have a 28-year-old female on her own buy a property. It didn't happen often. Nowadays when you put a well-located, beautifully designed apartment block on the market, the first 10 apartments will be sold to single career women.

Little inner-city terraces are also popular with this market segment. From my experience, women are often very good at visualising the potential of a property. They tend to have great intuition and a sixth sense about good properties and good locations. Single career women have proven extremely adroit at selecting growth locations and adding value.

Ones to watch – Sydney

Top capital growth suburbs in 2005 in Sydney include:

* Botany/Mascot
* Concord West
* Cromer
* Erskineville
* Hornsby
* Kogarah
* Petersham
* Rhodes
* Warriewood
* West Pymble

DRIVE-BY INVESTING

My strong preference is to buy an investment property you can drive past. If you're investing in an area near where you live or work, you will have a much better sense of the location and it will be easier to pick the best properties. The initial acquisition is far less risky if the property is in a location that you can thoroughly research.

Sure, you can do a lot of research on the Internet, but there's nothing like spending a few weekends driving around, looking at every open-for-inspection, getting to know a few agents, and immersing yourself in the search. Now, if you live in Sydney and you're trying to buy a property in Brisbane, it's going to be a hell of a lot harder to do that.

The other consideration is, should anything go wrong – a six-week vacancy, the roof starts leaking, there's a burglary, etc. – it's much easier to deal with if you're nearby. You can inspect the property and meet with the managing agent if need be. I don't believe real estate is an ideal remote investment. You don't have to be totally hands-on, but I think it should be accessible to you.

Having said that, if there's no capital growth happening near where you live and work, obviously you'll need to look further afield. You may not be able to afford a property in your stomping ground, but there's probably a good buy nearby.

BUYING THE RIGHT PROPERTY

In Australia, 67 per cent of homes are owner-occupied. Thus, owner-occupiers create the lion's share of demand for residential property. Since our goal is to buy in-demand property, it makes sense to buy a home that will appeal to owner-occupiers, because they make up two-thirds of the buyers.

A property with features that appeal to owner-occupiers will always return better capital growth than a generic apartment in a B-grade block that has been marketed to investors. It will also be more appealing to tenants, which helps maximise your rent and reduces the risk of vacancies. Plus it will be easier to sell in any market, which further reduces your risk.

What to buy?

The guiding rule for investors is: buy what owner-occupiers want to buy.

If it feels good ...

A lot of books on property investment advise you to be totally passionless when deciding what property to buy. It's all about the numbers, they say. I disagree. There's definitely a science of property investment – researching locations, getting the best finance and organising your cash flow. But there's also room for your intuition and feelings when you select the property.

I often advise people to buy an investment property that feels good for them. Imagine if a friend or family member was considering renting this property, and they asked for your opinion. What would you tell them? Does it have a livable layout? Is it light and airy? Is it secure? Is it in a pleasant neighbourhood? Would you feel good about them living there?

Be emotion*less* when it comes to negotiating the deal. But you can afford to let your good feelings guide you when it comes to choosing the property. I think that most people should be able to trust their intuition.

TENANTS' LIKES AND DISLIKES

From a capital-growth point of view, you want to buy something that appeals to owner-occupiers. But never lose sight of the fact that you need the rental income to fund the investment. Make sure the property you buy suits the tenants in the area. Here are some typical tenant likes and dislikes.

Close, but not too close

Tenants like to be close to shopping centres, schools, medical centres, cafés and restaurants, and entertainment and sporting facilities, but they don't like to be right next door to them. Few people want to live next door to a factory, public toilet or police station either.

Getting out and about

Close proximity to public transport and arterial roads is a bonus. But there's a trade-off between easy access to transport and the pollution it creates. Tenants don't mind having a bus stop outside their front door, but they don't want a railway line over the back fence.

Pleasant environment

Neighbourhoods with established trees, leafy streets, aesthetically pleasing architecture, beaches and waterways, parks and green space, and plenty of fresh air are always popular with tenants. Keep well clear of industrial zones, aircraft flight paths, sewerage plants, rubbish dumps, electricity substations and major powerlines. Be aware of noise pollution from roads, pubs and clubs, and garbage trucks servicing commercial properties.

The importance of aspect

The aspect of the property is a very important part of capital growth. You can always change the décor of a property, but you can never change the location or the orientation. In Australia people pay a premium for a northerly orientation of the main living, family and garden areas. If you can secure an investment property in a nice location with a northern orientation, that's really got capital growth stamped all over it.

HOUSE OR APARTMENT?

People often ask me, 'What's a better investment — a house or an apartment?' The correct answer depends on your lifestyle and your budget. If you're looking for low maintenance and a cheaper entry price, obviously an apartment is going to fit the bill. But if you're looking for something with better growth potential, and you're willing to do a bit of maintenance, a house is a better choice.

The big upside of houses is that their value typically grows faster than apartments. If you buy a house that's a bit older and needs a little bit of rejuvenation work, you can generally add value quickly and early, if you choose to. My advice is to buy a good house if you can afford to, otherwise buy the best apartment you can.

While houses have traditionally had greater capital growth than apartments, the gap is closing. Inner-city apartments are increasingly popular due to their close proximity to the CBD and their superior security. Developers have lifted their game and there is a new breed of well-designed apartment which incorporates outdoor living areas and shared leisure facilities.

The obvious advantages of apartments for the investor are that the entry price is lower and the owners' corporation takes care of maintenance of the building. Demand is also in favour of apartments, as 70 per cent of tenants rent apartments.

You'll also find that apartments tend to have fewer vacancies. Having said that, as I write this Sydney and Melbourne have just been through apartment construction booms. There's a bit of a glut, and vacancies are high. But, generally speaking, apartments are quicker and easier to rent than houses.

Ratio of owner-occupiers to tenants

If you're going to buy an apartment, it's worth finding out the ratio of owner-occupiers to tenants in the block. Owner-occupiers exact less wear and tear on the common areas of a building due to their pride of ownership and lower turnover. So to minimise maintenance costs and the possibilities of more vacancies, or having to lower rent because the building is looking shabby, I would choose a building that has at least 70 per cent owner-occupiers.

Size counts

When it comes to houses, your tenants are more likely to be families. A three-bedroom house offers the flexibility of having children's bedrooms and/or a home office. A two-bedroom home is a good proposition for couples, small families or shared households. As families tend to be smaller these days, if you buy a four-bedroom house, you're going to have a slimmer market and might find it harder to rent.

CONDITION

One of the beauties of buying an established property in a prime location is that you have the ability to add value. If you're a little bit more adventurous and you're prepared to put some time and money into renovating, buying an established property will often give you a better return.

While you can quickly add value by rejuvenating an investment property, I wouldn't buy a house that needs a total renovation. By doing so you're increasing both your risks and the acquisition costs. You have to fork out for designers, builders and materials, and you won't have any rent coming in while the work is carried out. There may be issues with local councils, and renovations have a habit of extending way beyond their original deadline. All this eats into your cash flow.

You should familiarise yourself with the costs of a quick rejuvenation. There are so many home-renovation television shows on now, you can easily educate yourself from the couch! By spending a few thousand dollars on fresh paint and carpet, you can generally attract a better-quality tenant who will be prepared to pay a little bit more rent to get something better.

I'm talking about a light makeover, not a total upgrade. If you have to spend more than 5 per cent of the purchase price to get the home into a rentable state, I'd probably look elsewhere.

Beware of overcapitalising

A small outlay for a cosmetic makeover can pay relatively greater returns than a big-budget renovation.

We manage nearly 3000 properties of all different types on behalf of investors. And I have to say, there is significantly more maintenance on period homes than there is on newer property. If you buy a terrace or a semi, you need to be prepared for ongoing maintenance costs. For people who want an absolute headache-free, maintenance-free investment, you're better off buying something newer.

NEW VS OLD

One of the big advantages of buying a newly constructed investment property is that you can claim depreciation on the building as a tax-deductible expense. For buildings constructed after 15 September 1987, the Australian Taxation Office allows you to write off 2.5 per cent of the original cost of construction of the building each year.

The deduction can give a significant boost to your cash flow position. If you want to claim this deduction, you'll need a valuation of the building from a quantity surveyor. If you're buying a brand new home, the developer should supply you with a quantity surveyor's valuation. Make sure this is included in your contract of sale.

While you're almost certain to have some maintenance issues with an older property, it would be a mistake to believe that a new property will be totally free of defects. Freshly finished décor can hide a multitude of sins. That's why you must get a proper building inspection on new homes as well as old. A trained eye will be able to pick up any potential problems.

Older may be better

Buying an apartment that is 5 to 10 years old may be a better bet than buying brand new. You'll be able to find out about the building's history, and any construction problems will probably have been ironed out. Also, you know who the neighbours will be.

TRAPS FOR NEW PLAYERS

There are a few things less experienced property investors should pay attention to when selecting a property. Bathrooms and kitchens are expensive to rectify or update, so make sure those rooms are in good condition and reasonably tastefully decorated.

In my rental management days, I used to have a building in Bondi Road where the owner, for reasons known only to himself, put in orange kitchens throughout the building. Perhaps he got a good deal on them, or orange was his favourite colour. In any case, the apartments always used to take three times longer than anything else to rent.

I'd always cringe when prospective tenants went into the kitchen, because I'd either hear a shriek or stony silence. I'd be in the lounge room, crossing my fingers and hoping maybe they were colour blind. They'd usually come out and say, 'Thanks very much, but it's not for us'.

You don't need to have state-of-the-art kitchens and bathrooms, but you have to be careful that they're not offensive to anyone. Because that'll make the property harder to rent, and it'll probably mean you'll have to significantly update it before you sell, which could be a major cost.

NEUTRAL DÉCOR, SECURE AND LOW MAINTENANCE

Low-maintenance properties are good for rentals because tenants are usually not inclined to do a lot of external maintenance, such as gardening, mowing the lawn, cleaning pools and so forth. Don't buy something with an exotic African garden in the back, because it's probably going to be dead in six months.

In most major cities, security is a major concern for tenants. So for apartments you'll need to consider the location of entrances and lifts, and the position of the apartment in the building. I would tend to steer away from ground-floor and possibly even first-floor apartments. If you can get something higher up, it gives tenants a sense of security, and you're less likely to be fixing break-ins and putting bars on windows.

Your décor should be simple and neutral. If it's not that way already, you may need to change it. Tenants are unlikely to want to spend much of their own money painting, decorating and changing window coverings. A tenant wants to put their furniture in and start living without having to worry if their sofa is going to clash with the embossed red wallpaper.

PRICE RANGE

I recommend buying a property that's 10 to 20 per cent above the average price of a home in that suburb. An average home in an in-demand area will likely yield good capital growth. But a slightly more expensive house is likely to have more desirable features and be more in-demand, and thus yield superior growth.

The difference in funding an investment property worth $400 000 versus $350 000 will often not be that much when you take into account the higher rental you receive. And those extra features – a garage or district views, for example – may mean an extra 1 per cent growth, which can make a big difference over time.

In demand

If someone said to me, 'I just bought a house at auction. I had to outbid 10 people and I paid $30 000 above the reserve', I'd feel pleased for them because they've bought an in-demand property. If they secured it for a reasonable price, they're probably in for a fantastic ride with capital growth.

Ones to watch – Melbourne

If you're buying for capital growth in Melbourne in 2005, here are some blue-chip and up-and-coming suburbs which I consider good bets:

* Albert Park
* Brighton
* Canterbury
* Cheltenham
* Frankston
* Hawthorn
* Kensington
* Toorak
* Williamstown
* Yarraville

THE RIGHT FINANCE

An investment property requires a different finance strategy than buying your home. While you still want to find the lowest interest rate you can, you need to structure your loan differently to maximise leverage and tax concessions.

I recommend using interest-only loans to buy your investment property. Because you're not making any contributions to the principle during the course of the loan, your repayments are less. This maximises your cash flow and allows you to buy more property.

The principal portion of principal and interest loan repayments is not a tax-deductible expense. So even though you're increasing your equity in the property, the principal repayments are, in essence, dead money. You can build your net worth faster with capital growth from buying more property with interest-only loans.

AVOID IF POSSIBLE

Despite all its advantages, residential property investment is not a foolproof way to make money. You need to develop an understanding of the market, do your research, buy the right property, and be patient while you let capital growth take effect. Because you're buying for growth, the most important decision is which property to buy. Here are some properties to avoid.

'Bargain' second-tier city locations

You sometimes see ads for apartment blocks targeted at investors. On paper they sound great – brand new, two bedrooms, two bathrooms, balcony, security car space, inner-city location, $340 000. The pricing is very keen. Sounds like a bargain, but be cautious. If something looks too good to be true, then it probably is.

Once you get over the lure of the low asking price, you'll soon realise these blocks are in inferior locations that don't appeal to owner-occupiers. There will be little growth in the long run. The reason the pricing is so keen is because the developer's bought the site cheaply as no one wanted it, and/or they've been able to get away with inferior fixtures and fittings.

Rental guarantees

A rental guarantee is where a developer guarantees an incoming purchaser a certain minimum rent for an initial period. The developer will subsidise any shortfall from the guaranteed amount. You'll see a big headline in the ad 'Guaranteed 7 per cent per annum for the next five years'.

Rental guarantees are often used by developers to justify inflated prices. It's not uncommon for the rent to drop when the rental guarantee period expires, leaving you with a big hole in your budget. At that point you have to live with the market rent and make that cash flow work.

My view is that an investment property should be able to stand on its own two feet. If someone has to guarantee the rent, then it's probably not a sustainable, realistic rent. If it's not sustainable and realistic, it means you're probably paying a premium price based on that. So I'm a great believer in just letting the market rent flow through.

Serviced apartments

Serviced apartments are a bit like hotel suites without the room service and housekeeping. They're popular with business people and holiday-makers for short or long stays. Investing in a serviced apartment carries a lot more risk than buying a house or an apartment. You're relying on the operator to get it right, and on the tourism and business markets to remain strong. With apartments and houses, on the other hand, there's always demand from people wanting to rent.

By definition, the resale market for serviced apartments is confined to investors. So you're restricted to a much smaller resale market. Since growth generally comes from owner-occupiers, if you buy a property that can only ever be used as an investment, it's not going to have the same growth potential either. The market for serviced apartments is still untested in most parts of Australia.

Refurbished commercial property

A building that has been purpose-built for commercial or industrial use doesn't always work well as a residential space. Compromises often have to be made with floor plans, leaving apartment owners with unworkable rooms and wasted space.

Also, the biggest problems I've encountered with owners' corporations have arisen from structural defects in retro-fitted commercial buildings. They all look great on day one, but after a couple of years they're often beginning to show problems. There's been a lot of structural cracking in the walls and ceilings, and I've known a lot of buildings in the city that have had major leaks.

Company title apartments

Company title buildings often have bylaws restricting owners' rights to rent their apartments. They can range from a total prohibition to the prospective tenants being vetted by an owners' committee. With so much strata title property to choose from, there's no need to put yourself in a position where you have to jump through these hoops each time you get a new tenant.

A TALE OF TWO INVESTORS

Peter, a good friend of mine, came to see me in 2000, before the Sydney Olympics. He'd put away $40 000 and he said to me, 'What should I do with my money?' I said, 'Right, let's find you a property.' I recommended he secure the best thing he could afford at that time. So I found him a little terrace in inner-city Ultimo for $290 000.

It needed a little bit of fixing up, but he could have put a tenant straight in there. It was in a part of Sydney that I believed was likely to outpace the rest of the market. Ultimo wasn't too trendy or popular at that point, but it is on the doorstep of the city, and I felt it had the potential of being another Paddington down the track.

But Peter got cold feet. There had been a lot of talk about the market going flat after the Olympics. He was a bit concerned about that, and he also felt he needed to save a bigger deposit. So he decided to wait a little while and attempt to save some more funds.

UP, UP AND AWAY

What in fact happened was that the market started to escalate quite rapidly. Peter found, as people often do, that the price of property went up far faster than he could save. He got a little bit disenchanted with the market, and he never really got into buying mode. He never got out of consideration mode.

In the meantime I recommended the Ultimo property to another friend, Michael, who bought it. He spent around $40 000 on a renovation, putting in a new kitchen and bathroom. A few years later he asked me to sell the terrace for him and we sold it for $590 000 at auction.

At around the same time Peter came to see me again. He said, 'Look I've been thinking about this property thing. I know I missed the boat last time but I'd like to consider it again.' And I said, 'How much have you got?' And he said, 'Forty thousand.' Unfortunately, Pete's deposit would only buy him half the property it would have bought him a few years earlier.

TAKING ACTION

If there's a lesson to be learnt from this story, it's about the power of making a decision and taking action. There are a lot of people who hesitate in the property market. And while you shouldn't rush in foolishly, you need to be prepared to take up an opportunity when it arises, because they don't last forever.

When you buy investment property, there's a huge amount of excitement and a small sense of fear. It's natural to be cautious. After all, it's a big amount of money, a big commitment, and a big obligation to repay. But don't let your fear prevail. There is some degree of risk in any investment.

Here are a few quick tips to help you get started:

✳ Organise your loan and your cash flow before you start looking.

✳ Identify what is the most suitable property for you.

✳ Finally, get started as soon as possible, because it's costing you 10 per cent per annum to wait.

DOING THE NUMBERS

After you've found some suitable investment properties, you need to work out your cash flow to see whether you can afford to own one. A common error made by rookie property investors is underestimating the costs of owning the property in the long run. Owning an investment property comes down to your ability to cover the ongoing costs.

One of my guiding principles of property investment is to keep it simple. However, it's essential that you understand the cash flow and make sure you can afford to cover the shortfall between the rent and the expenses. It's easy to put together a simple spreadsheet with your rent and expenses, or you can get your accountant or bookkeeper to do it for you.

Successful property investors take a businesslike approach – they minimise the costs, maximise the revenue (i.e. the rent) and keep a close eye on the cash flow. If you've bought well and are taking a long-term approach, you can be confident the upside will look after itself.

RENT – YOUR REVENUE

Before you buy an investment property, you should familiarise yourself with the rents in the area so you'll know how much you're likely to receive for any property you are contemplating buying. A good place to start your research is on a real estate Internet portal. You can search any area for any type of property and see what the current rents are. You can also talk to agents and property managers who operate in the area.

You also need to factor in vacancy rates when you're doing your cash flow calculations. You can check what the vacancy rate is for the area with the Real Estate Institute in your state. Typically, you should factor in around about 3 to 5 per cent vacancy, or roughly two to three weeks a year. (To calculate the vacancy rate in weeks per year, divide the vacancy percentage by two e.g. 3 per cent vacancy = 1.5 vacant weeks per year.)

You also need to keep pace with the current market rentals. While you definitely want to look after your tenants, you owe it to yourself as an investor to get an appropriate return on your money. Get your managing agent to advise you, at least once a year, if the rent can be moved up a bit.

Setting the rent

Whatever you do, don't overprice your property. Usually the only tenants who will pay an over-market rent are people who have been knocked back from other properties. Or they make an application as a couple and they end up having two or three extra people move in with them. (This is not necessarily legal, by the way, but it happens.)

You'll also find that you'll have a higher turnover of tenants. People will sign the lease and their friends will say, 'What are you paying?' When your tenants tell them, their friends will say, 'Well, I'm only paying [some figure less than what you're asking] ... you're paying too much.' So as soon as the lease is up, your tenants move out.

I recommend small, regular increases in rent. Some landlords don't put the rent up for two years and then try and put it up by $50 a week. Tenants don't like that. Depending on what the market's doing, I would suggest perhaps a $5 to $10 increase in rent every 6 to 12 months. Just keep the rent ticking over, but not outpacing the market.

The season of the tenant

Don't sign leases that end around Christmas, because it's hard to find a new tenant between 1 December and 1 February. Everyone's on holidays, already made their move or they're not going to make their move until the new year, so you can end up with an extended vacancy. If you're drawing up a lease around Christmas, make it for 11 or 14 months, so it expires outside the holiday period.

The demand for rental properties in some locations fluctuates seasonally. For example, there's usually more demand for beachside properties in summer than in winter. If you're in a seasonal location, make sure your lease doesn't expire in a down period, because you might have to lower the rent to attract a tenant.

That doesn't mean a beachside tenant can't go onto a month-by-month lease after the lease expires and leave in winter. But if someone moves in around March, you would probably want to give them a nine-month lease. Often tenants start thinking about moving when their lease expires – they don't usually have to move, but they often start thinking about it.

COSTS

Now you have a handle on the income, you need to estimate the expenses. The costs of owning an investment property are as follows.

Interest

Interest on your loan is the single biggest expense for most property investors.

Accounting and bookkeeper's fees

I recommend hiring an accountant to make sure you get the maximum deductions and stay abreast of the latest tax rules. A bookkeeper frees up your time and keeps detailed financial records and depreciation schedules for your accountant.

Advertising

You may need to place ads in the newspaper or on the Internet to attract some tenants.

Strata levies

Strata levies vary hugely, depending on the age and condition of the building and its facilities. They can cost anything from $300 to $3000 or more per quarter.

Rates

You'll have to pay the council and local water authority quarterly rates for the services they provide.

Maintenance and upkeep

You should set aside a fund for keeping your property in good condition. Maintenance can include everything from touching up the paintwork to putting on a new roof. You may also have to pay for mowing the lawn and tidying up the garden from time to time.

Insurance

It's essential to protect your investment with the appropriate insurance, which includes building, contents, public liability, workers' compensation and loss of rent due to damage. Some landlords' insurance packages combine all of these – speak to your insurance broker.

Land tax

Land tax is levied as a percentage of the value of the land only (not including any buildings) and varies from state to state. You must pay it annually.

Pest control

The last thing you want is to have your investment eaten away by white ants, so you'll need periodic pest inspections.

Property management fees

Agent's fees typically comprise:

* a commission on all the rent paid – most agents across Australia charge 7 per cent;

* a fee for finding a tenant – often equal to one week's rent;

* some agreements include advertising, otherwise you'll have to pay for it – I'd rather give an agent a budget of $100 or $200 to put a couple of ads in the local and metro papers to get a tenant quickly, instead of trying to negotiate a zero fee where you're in the hands of the agent as to how much they want to advertise;

* a small fee for preparing leases;

* sundries, such as photocopying, stamp duty, postage, etc.

TAX ISSUES

The government has given real estate a generous array of tax deductions that can reduce your tax burden and make it easier to buy an investment property. The costs of owning negatively geared property exceed the rental income received from it. In other words, the property is making a loss. For taxation purposes, you can deduct this loss against income you earn from other sources, e.g. your salary.

The net effect is that your tax burden is lessened. If you earn $60 000, your marginal rate of tax is 42 per cent (2004/2005 rates). Consequently any tax deductions from your negatively geared property result in a tax refund at the same rate of 42 per cent. In effect there are three people paying for your investment property: you, your tenant and the taxman.

Watch your deductions like a hawk

To maximise the return from your property, you must claim all your tax deductions. Many property investors short-change themselves by claiming less back from the taxman than they are entitled to. As well as all the cash expenses I have outlined above, you can also claim a deduction for depreciation. Tax deductions for depreciation help your rental income to go further, minimising the cost of owning the property.

Deductions for deprecation arise in two areas. Firstly there is depreciation on the building. Homes are depreciable over 40 years, so you're entitled to claim 2.5 per cent of the cost of the building as a tax deduction every year. You can also claim a depreciation allowance on capital improvements such as garages, new kitchens and extensions.

You can also deduct depreciation on fittings and fixtures such as carpets, curtains, hot water heaters and dishwashers. The best way to maximise the deductible depreciation on fixtures and fittings is to get a depreciation schedule drawn up by a quantity surveyor. They're up to date on the latest tax rulings and are like bloodhounds when it comes to finding items to depreciate.

Keeping afloat

The good news for negatively geared property investors is that they don't have to wait until the end of the year to claim their tax back. By filling out a form with the Australian Taxation Office, you can have your PAYG withholding rate adjusted to reflect your true income situation.

Suppose you own an investment property and you estimate that the annual cash loss will be $6000. Your annual gross income from your employer is $55 000. Therefore, your estimated taxable income will be $49 000 ($55 000 less $6000). You can apply for a variation to have your withholding rate recalculated based on your estimated taxable income of $49 000.

You then have more money in your pay packet each period, which you can use immediately to pay the costs of owning the property. If you want to vary your withholding rate, you need to lodge a PAYG income tax withholding variation application form with the Australian Taxation Office. Talk to the ATO or your accountant for more details.

Worth their weight in gold

As with all tax matters, it pays to employ a good accountant to make sure you claim everything you're entitled to.

GET THE OWNERSHIP RIGHT

When you buy an investment property, you have to decide who will own it. It can be owned by you solely or jointly with another person, or by a company, trust or superannuation fund. Ownership can have far-reaching legal, control and tax implications. Getting it right from the start can save you a lot of hassle in the future.

There are four questions to ask yourself:

1. Who do I want to be in control?

2. How can I minimise income tax now and capital gains later?

3. What will happen if the owner dies or if the joint owners separate?

4. How will I protect my financial position if the holder of the investment gets into financial difficulty?

Sole ownership

This is the easiest and most straightforward way of owning an investment property. You have total control over the property and pay tax on any income at your personal marginal tax rate.

If you're buying a property with your partner, you can maximise the benefits of negative gearing if you put the property in the name of the highest taxpayer. That's because the Australian Taxation Office effectively subsidises tax-deductible expenditure at the marginal tax rate. So the higher the owner's marginal rate, the bigger the tax breaks. The catch is that capital gains tax is also levied at the marginal rate, so the highest earner will pay more if the property is sold.

Conversely, if the property has a positive cash flow, it's best to put in the name of the lowest taxpayer to minimise your tax liability.

Joint ownership

There are two ways to own a property jointly with others. You can be joint tenants, which means you own the property in equal shares. If one joint tenant dies, the surviving joint tenants automatically get that share, irrespective of the terms of any will.

Tenants in common can own the property in any proportions they like. If one dies, their share is passed on according to their will. Thus tenancy in common is well suited to friends or relatives owning property together, or for parents who want to leave their property to their children.

With joint ownership, expenses and income can be allocated according to shares, and you have an opportunity for income splitting and tax deductions for all. However, if the relationship breaks down, it can be expensive and difficult to untangle yourself.

Sole ownership is best

Nine times out of ten, sole ownership of investment property is the best way to minimise tax and maximise gains. Obviously there must be total trust between partners if the property is to be owned in only one party's name. If you're considering joint ownership, you should check with your accountant before you buy the property to see which structure will be most beneficial.

PROPERTY MANAGERS - THE INVESTOR'S BEST FRIEND

For first-time investors, managing the property yourself is a terrific learning experience. If you have the time, you'll certainly gain a hell of a lot of knowledge in a short period. But when it comes to the less pleasant management issues, such as increasing the rent or enforcing the rules, it's much less hassle to have someone else do it for you.

The benefits of having a good property manager far outweigh the costs, which are fully tax-deductible anyway. A good manager will help you to reduce vacancies and minimise the risk of damage to the property, and ensure you receive the maximum rental.

One of the most compelling reasons to use a property manager is that they're skilled at picking good tenants – those who will stay for the long term and not cause any problems. Not many investors have this skill, and it's usually acquired only after some bitter experiences. A manager will also be able to let the property faster, because they'll have a large selection of tenants on their database.

Finding a good property manager is like finding a good selling agent. You want to choose the best one, not the cheapest one. Make your selection based on the agent who you think is going to give you and your property the best service. The difference between a good agent and a bad agent can amount to thousands of dollars over the period of ownership.

Benefits of a good property manager

* You'll receive unbiased third-party advice about how to get the most out of your investment.

* They take care of unpleasant tasks such as raising the rent and enforcing rules.

* They have a database of prospective tenants so they can get your property rented more quickly.

* They know what décor and fixtures appeal to tenants, and they can suggest renovations and upgrades to get premium rents.

* Property managers often have deals with tradespeople who'll give you a more competitive rate because of the volume of the work the managers refer to them.

* They'll make sure your rent is maintained at market levels.

* Property managers can often be a conduit to future investment properties.

* They'll make sure your property is properly maintained and insured.

KEEPING YOUR TENANTS HAPPY

A friend of mine has a great strategy for keeping his residential property portfolio tenanted. He often sends his tenants small gifts – a bottle of champagne or flowers – at Christmas or when they move in. He makes a little effort to build a great relationship with his tenants and consequently they generally all pay their rent on time and look after his properties.

Your tenants are actually an asset in your property investment 'business', so it's in your interest to keep them happy. A couple of nice little surprises to maintain a positive relationship with someone who's paying you $25 000 a year in rent is money well spent.

Make sure repairs are carried out promptly. I've had tenants come to us after they've quit a property based on the fact they had a window that didn't open and they asked the agent to get it fixed three times but nothing happened. So the tenant got annoyed and moved out, and the landlord's potentially got a four-week vacancy just become someone didn't spend $50 promptly to get the window fixed.

MANAGING RISKS

No investment is without risks, and residential property certainly has its fair share. Fortunately it's relatively easy to manage and minimise these risks. Here's how.

Vacancies

Nothing will zap your profits faster than vacancies. You must take precautions to limit them as much as possible. Firstly, make sure you buy a good property. In-demand property in desirable locations is rarely vacant. A good property manager will have plenty of tenants on their books and can minimise vacancies between tenants.

Make sure the rent is set at the market and not above it, and the property is kept in spic-and-span condition. Because if you have a $400 a week property vacant for two months, that will cost you $3200. Whereas you might find that steam cleaning the carpets and giving it a fresh coat of paint at a cost of $1500 will help you get a good tenant in quickly. You might also be able to charge a bit more rent.

A long-term vacancy in residential property is not usually a big problem because average vacancy rates are around 3 to 5 per cent (which amounts to one to three weeks' vacancy per year). But these figures are the average – some properties are vacant for longer periods, while others are not vacant at all. That's why it's crucial to buy the right property in the first place.

If your property is consistently vacant for long periods, you have to find out why. It may be overpriced or substandard for the area. The worst-case scenario is that the property is a dog and will be perennially unpopular with tenants. If that's the case, you should seriously consider cutting your losses and selling.

Interest rate rises

Because property investment is a long-term proposition, you can expect interest rates to fluctuate over the period of ownership. Since interest is usually the biggest expense, you have to be careful that an interest hike doesn't put you in a precarious financial position.

The best way to protect yourself from an interest rate rise is to get a fixed interest rate mortgage. You might end up paying a little more over the course of the loan, but it will give you peace of mind.

Also, look at your leverage. The more equity you have in the property, the bigger buffer you have against interest rate rises. You can always refinance the property to a higher LVR (loan-to-value ratio) to cover the cost of an interest rate increase.

Building repairs

When it comes to repairs and maintenance, prevention is always better than cure. Make sure you inspect your property regularly to nip any potential structural defects in the bud. You might even consider getting a building inspector in from time to time to give your property a thorough checkup. A small repair left undone can become a big headache in a few years time.

Property managers will usually inspect your property on your behalf twice a year and give you a written inspection report. When you receive the report, it's a good time to ring the manager and talk about any necessary repairs and maintenance issues. Or you can always accompany the manager on the inspection and see for yourself.

A lot of landlords don't want to spend money on their properties and so some managers are a little bit hesitant to recommend repairs and maintenance. I would be inclined to be a little bit proactive in this department, and encourage the manager to give you timely recommendations on things that need attention and improvements that will maximise the rent.

The landlord's enemy number one

In my experience in property management, I'd say that water is the major enemy of the landlord, whether it's natural weather penetration, rising damp or a leaking roof. You need to keep your property watertight. Get your roof checked on a regular basis, because a small leak in the roof today could lead to a new roof, new ceiling and new joists being required in two years' time.

In heavy storms, small leaks in windows can lead to all sorts of damp in the brickwork and paintwork, and damage carpet. Rising damp can be an issue, especially for Victorian-era terraces. A building inspection upfront will give you an idea of whether there's going to be any rising damp issues in the walls and, if so, what the cost of rectification is likely to be.

Termites are also attracted to damp areas such as underneath a laundry with a leaking washing machine. Get regular pest inspections, because a termite infestation could potentially cost you tens of thousands of dollars.

Cash buffer

It's always a good idea to have a cash buffer for contingencies. You don't want to be caught short if interest rates go up a quarter of a per cent or you have a four-week vacancy. I also suggest setting aside 5 to 10 per cent of your annual income as a sinking fund for periodic building maintenance.

Damage by the tenant

Even with the most careful selection, there is always the risk the tenant will maliciously or negligently damage your property. For a few hundred dollars you can get landlord's insurance that will cover the cost of repairs if the tenant trashes your property. You're usually covered for the loss of rent for the period it takes to do the repairs as well.

In my experience the major risk for investors is tenant damage, so you definitely shouldn't compromise on tenant selection. Ensure your manager has done thorough reference checks, and consider a personal interview with the tenant the manager recommends. It's like handing them the keys to a Rolls-Royce, so you want to make sure they're going to take good care of it.

Don't risk it

Landlord's insurance covers you for most of the common risks of owning an investment property, including:

✳ the tenant defaulting on the rent or doing a runner

✳ accidental and malicious damage to your property and theft

✳ lost rent while damage is repaired.

NO OR LOW CAPITAL GROWTH

It would be irresponsible for me to suggest to you that all property goes up in value all the time. That's simply not the case. Property values don't rise continuously in a straight line. They tend to stagnate for a while before a boom period, when they rise rapidly, before returning to a plateau. That's why I recommend property investment as a long-term proposition.

If your property isn't growing as much as you'd like, you first need to assess whether the market is in a flat spell. If so, a little bit of patience could pay off. A few more years and you could be enjoying accelerated growth.

However, if the property market is in an upswing but your property's value is stagnant, rents are flat and it's costing you money and stress, it may be time to move on. If you assess the situation as unlikely to improve, you're better off selling the property and freeing up the funds for better investments.

An underperforming property usually comes down to insufficient research and bad selection. It's better to sell and cut your losses, figure out where you went wrong and resolve to do better next time, rather than hang in there in the vain hope it will turn around.

INCREASING YOUR CAPITAL

One of the great beauties of property investment is that it's easy to add value to your investment. Perhaps the quickest and easiest ways to increase your capital is to take a structurally sound but daggy or untidy property and give it a makeover.

The trick is to add more in perceived value than you actually spend on renovating. Your goal is to add the wow factor without blowing the budget. My top 10 ways to add value to your investment property without spending a lot of money are as follows.

1. Paint

The options are endless – outside, inside, the trim, the roof, the front door, fences, ceilings, the shed, etc. Nothing lifts the look and feel of a home better than a fresh coat of paint.

2. Build a carport

Providing accommodation for your tenant's car will not only add value to your property, but you'll be able to increase the rent by around $20 per week as well.

3. New curtains or blinds

New window coverings not only improve the décor, they also add privacy.

4. Install a skylight

This is a quick and inexpensive way to bring more natural light into dark houses.

5. Replace light fittings

For a small outlay you can modernise the look of your property with new light fittings. Why not update the light switches while you're at it?

6. Put in a barbecue

No Australian home should be without a barbecue. They can turn a dull back yard into an outdoor entertaining area, especially with the addition of some paving and a pergola.

7. Steam clean carpets

Carpet cleaning can dramatically improve the condition of a dirty carpet and remove odours.

8. Sand the floorboards

If the carpet is beyond repair, you can rip it up and have the floorboards sanded and polished for a clean, contemporary look.

9. Replace door handles and knobs

This minor change can make a big impact. Make sure you do the kitchen cupboards as well.

10. Install a dishwasher

Tenants will appreciate it (and will be willing to pay a higher rent as well) and you can depreciate it for the taxman.

FINAL THOUGHTS

N ow you've reached the end of this book it's time to take some action, whether it's drawing up a weekly household budget so you can start saving for a deposit, arranging a few interviews with agents to list your home for sale, or talking to a mortgage manager about finance to buy an investment property.

The power of an idea is in its implementation. So the real benefit of the information I've supplied you throughout this book lies in your ability to take action upon it. No doubt you'll have some fears. Buying a home will probably be the biggest financial transaction of your life. So don't expect to grab this book and run into the marketplace without any fear or hesitation.

You should definitely sit down and carefully assess your position. Consider the purpose of your purchase. Look realistically at your current financial situation. Get together with your financial adviser or a mentor and work out how much you can afford to spend. Don't overstretch yourself, but be prepared to break through the fear barrier and take action when an opportunity presents itself.

Most of the risks in buying property can be minimised and managed. Building reports, market research, fixed interest rate loans, competent advisers – all these things go towards making a better-quality decision. And remember: your next purchase may not be your ultimate home or investment, but it can be a great stepping stone to the next level.

It's never the wrong time to make a good investment

There's an old saying in real estate that goes:

> When is the best time to buy property? Twenty years ago.
>
> When's the next best time to buy property? Today.

While there are definitely cycles in the property market, well-located, in-demand property rarely declines in value. Property investors should be aware of market cycles and track them. But often it's more a question of should you expect 3 per cent growth this year or 15 per cent growth this year?

If you view property as a medium- to long-term investment and buy in the established growth markets, you'll find it hard not to make good returns. And as I said earlier in the book, the feeling of making a good real estate investment or securing a home to live in, of taking the plunge and owning your own little piece of Australia, is a great confidence booster and will have other amazing benefits in your life.

Remember there's no such thing as the 'perfect property'. No one property will ever fit all the criteria you're looking for. The beauty, however, is that there are probably dozens of great potential new homes or investment properties that will work perfectly for you.

Good luck, and I look forward to hearing of your excitement and success in your property pursuits.

John McGrath, www.mcgrath.com.au